STAR
GAZING

STAR GAZING

The Players in My Life

RAVI SHASTRI

WITH

AYAZ MEMON

Illustrations by Shiva Rao

HarperCollins *Publishers* India

First published in India by
HarperCollins *Publishers* 2021
A-75, Sector 57, Noida, Uttar Pradesh 201301, India
www.harpercollins.co.in

2 4 6 8 10 9 7 5 3 1

P-ISBN: 978-93-5422-723-3
E-ISBN: 978-93-5422-454-6

Typeset in 13/17 Dante MT
Manipal Technologies Limited, Manipal

Printed and bound at
Thomson Press (India) Ltd

To the fans

CONTENTS

FRIENDS AND RIVALS

FROM THE BOX

INTRODUCTION

As a young boy, the name Garfield Sobers resonated with me deeply. My mother introduced me to him by gifting me a book, *Cricket Advance*, which he had written. My father followed up with stories of his all-round prowess. Sobers's amazing record, his style, his commitment to hard work – it all seemed magical. What a role model for a budding cricketer!

Sobers, as I learned later, had worked as an errand boy at a furniture factory in Barbados at the age of fourteen. He had also played cricket, using whatever was at hand, whenever he could – and become the world's greatest all-rounder.

The impact of Sobers and his genius on me is incalculable. I could never reach the same heights in my career, of course. Nobody has, in my opinion. He remains (for me) the most versatile and compelling cricketer of all time. He was my earliest inspiration when I took to cricket almost half a century ago.

But he's not been the only one.

As I grew into the sport, several other players also made an impression on me. The number increased when I started playing at the first-class and international levels, and has continued to do so throughout my years as commentator and coach.

Any sport thrives on heroes and role models whom fans want to watch, and up-and-coming athletes want to emulate. Their achievements become benchmarks for subsequent generations and inspire them to aim higher, which in turn sustains or grows a sport.

For instance, no batsman has been able to better Don Bradman's amazing run-getting, or batting average yet. I doubt anyone ever will. But Bradman has been like a beacon for every aspiring batsman of every generation – his own and since – to imitate.

The learning, if you are a student of the game, is never-ending, and not just restricted to skills and technique. As an eighteen-year-old youngster in the Indian dressing room, I was consumed by how Sunil Gavaskar prepared mentally for a match. At fifty-eight, and in the dressing room in an altogether different capacity, I find myself equally fascinated by how young Rishabh Pant – a complete contrast to Gavaskar in approach – primes himself for the challenges in the middle. Playing alongside a teenage Sachin Tendulkar in the early 1990s, I could only marvel at how smartly his mind worked on cricket tactics. Even back then, he seemed to be a nudge ahead in working out what the bowler was likely to do next, all quietly expressed. Now, as coach, Virat Kohli's bristling aggression has unerringly stoked the remaining fire in my belly too. He's not one to cede an inch on the ground, but it's not mindless bravado. He just loves to win. Off the field, he's a different person. Virat's capacity to compartmentalize his thoughts, switch on and off when required, is quite amazing. From Richie Benaud I learnt not only about cricket's nuances, but also why a clumsily knotted tie can put off TV audiences even if one is talking perfect sense. From Ian Chappell, apart from fantastic stories about eminent players – and the skills which made them great – I learnt that you have to carry your spine with you always, on the field or off it.

The thought of doing a book on cricketers – past and current – whom I've admired, enjoyed playing with/against or watching, and above all, learnt from in the past fifty years, came to me in late 2016, during one of my travels for a commentary assignment. I started jotting down names as a preliminary exercise, assuming that the number would be twenty-five or thereabouts. It turned out to be forty-two in the first go, and some names were still missing!

Fifty, I decided, was a good number to settle at, leaving eight names to be added for a second exercise. That didn't happen till after the 2019 World Cup. My responsibilities as chief coach after the ICC Champions Trophy in 2017 left me with little time to devote to this project. When I finally sat down to finalize the names, the list had swelled way past even fifty.

Months in lockdown because of the COVID-19 pandemic gave me the opportunity to fast-track the book. The players featured here are those who not only made runs and took wickets, but also influenced cricket in a big way and drew in more fans with their skills and accomplishments.

I've had to overlook some current stars like Rishabh Pant, Babar Azam, Marnus Labuschagne, Pat Cummins, Mohammed Shami, Cheteshwar Pujara, Jasprit Bumrah, Ajinkya Rahane – to name a few – but only because they are still building their body of work. I can see these and many other players featuring in my next collection!

There will, of course, be disagreements with the cricketers I've written about, and that's okay. All selectors must be sufficiently thick-skinned and prepared to take criticism.

GROWING UP

INTO THE

GAME

A LEAGUE OF HIS OWN

Garfield Sobers

The first I heard of Garfield Sobers was in my home in the early 1970s. Barely ten, I had begun to show some aptitude in both bowling and batting, which kind of impressed my father. 'We have a Sobers in the house,' he once declared jokingly to his friends who were visiting.

I hadn't seen Sobers play when the West Indies toured India in 1966-67, so for the first few years of my cricketing journey, his stupendous all-round skills were known to me only through hearsay. A great deal of it through my father, who was an unabashed fan.

Dad was a horse lover and when he spoke of Sobers, the word used often was 'pedigree'. He would show me photographs of the great West Indian, highlighting his sinewy physique, great sense of balance, batting or bowling, and the way he could draw so much power in whatever he did by making comparisons with pedigreed horses.

As my cricketing ambitions and education grew, I made it a point to learn more about Sobers. What I read – and subsequently saw on videos too – revealed an exceptional, multi-dimensional player who not only won matches on his own, but did so incomparably.

Videos and films give a more vivid expression to sporting action than still photographs, and Sobers's magnificent prowess came through tellingly. Tall and athletic, he batted with panache and timing that separates the great batsmen from the very good. He could bowl genuinely fast, fast-medium with late swing either way, or switch to orthodox left-arm spin when needed.

Super quick on his feet, Sobers could field in any position, and a strong left arm meant he could throw hard over long distances. After he became captain, he preferred to stand close-in to be more involved in the game, and his lightning reflexes and keen ball sense helped him take sensational catches.

Though most of the matches Sobers played go far in establishing his batting genius, two are particularly memorable. One was when he played for Nottinghamshire against Glamorgan at Swansea in his debut season in county cricket in 1968, and the other was in 1972 on a fiery Perth pitch as the Rest of the World took on Australia. I have watched these contests hundreds of times, as I am sure everyone from my fraternity and those who love and follow the game have done over the years. In the 1980s, it wasn't so easy to get footage, which is now readily available on YouTube etc., but the effort was worthwhile to understand Sobers's genius.

The match at Swansea was remarkable for Sobers's lusty hitting against Malcolm Nash. After the first three balls had been hit over the fence, high on adrenaline, he went for broke, hitting the next three for six too – becoming the first batsman in history to do so in one over.

His 254 against Australia is rightly considered a classic. It is extraordinary for the quality and range of strokes, which Sobers's bat spat out as a machine gun does bullets. A high backlift usually heightens the risk in batting, but also enhances the beauty of strokes, and Sobers was utterly, marvellously, delightfully in control in that knock. He made the Australia attack – Dennis Lillee, Bob Massie, Graeme Watson, Terry Jenner, Kerry O'Keeffe – seem positively mediocre, especially Lillee, whom he smashed ruthlessly.

I am hardly the type who gets overawed by anything or anyone, but when I first met Sobers in the flesh, on the tour to the West Indies in 1983, I could barely utter a word. I couldn't take my eyes off him, and barely registered what he said in his sing-song Barbadian accent. The splendid athlete I had seen on videos was now a man approaching middle age, with a hobbling gait that spoke of years of wear and tear on his knees from playing cricket relentlessly all over the world. Yet, he was still very much a superstar, though he wore his fame lightly.

When I found my voice, Sobers was helpful, giving me important tips on batting – I had by then got a promotion up the order – and spin bowling when I asked him how to improve. The abiding lesson: don't underestimate yourself, no matter the reputation of the opponent.

In January 1985, batting against Baroda at Bombay, I hit left-arm spinner Tilak Raj for six sixes in an over, which brought me

level with Sobers in this rare record. The heady feeling remained
with me till I reached home, where my father took me aside
briefly, away from all the congratulations and visitors.

'Fantastic, son, but remember, there can never be another
Gary Sobers.'

I had taken after my old man in being blunt, and our views
often clashed. But in this we were in complete agreement.

PLAY HARD, PLAY FAIR

Ian Chappell

 My first cricket hero was Gundappa Viswanath, but Ian Chappell is the one who I grew up idolizing after being initiated into the sport.

There was no TV coverage of overseas cricket in the early 1970s. Radio was the only real-time link to cricket action happening outside of India. I would be glued to Radio Australia whenever matches were played in that country, and this was my introduction to Chappell.

There was a buzz around him when he was playing. His name would crop up in the commentary more frequently than any other player's, even when he wasn't batting. The 1974-75 Ashes series tipped everything in Chappell's favour where I was concerned. His dashing approach as a batsman and hard aggression as captain made a huge impact on me.

From an early age, I found the so-called niceties of the game somewhat hypocritical. If you don't take the field to win, why play at all? Chappell was the kind of player I wanted to be. He was a polarizing figure in his heyday. He played really hard, but also played fair, as I got to understand, which seemed the best way to play.

I would read about how he would be in eyeball-to-eyeball confrontation with opponents on the field, then share a beer with the same person immediately after the game. This was 'spirit of cricket' for me, and made Chappell even more endearing.

He was obviously a fantastic captain, not losing a single series. He had the ability to get the best out of his players, and under him, Australia became world-beaters in the 1970s. It's not often that players are revered by teammates long after their playing days are over, but Chappell still commands the loyalty of those who played under him. This says something about his character and personal charisma.

I got to know Chappell on the several tours we made of Australia from the 1980s, and used these opportunities to pick his brain, get insights into why he was so successful as a captain. Essentially, as I understood, this was because he was always looking to take a match forward, not waiting for things to happen.

I got to know him better when we became fellow commentators for Mark Mascarenhas's WorldTel. Like me, Mark too admired Chappell hugely, and there were several evenings we spent discussing cricket's past, present and future.

He had the reputation of being abrasive, but that was far from the real Chappell as I discovered working with him. True, he could be as blunt as a shovel, irrespective of the reputation of the other party. But not pointlessly; only if he believed there was an absence of reason or misuse of position by the other.

I love his droll sense of humour too. It takes a while to get used to it because he is not the boisterous, guffawing kind. He has biting wit, and, with age, this has become even sharper.

When Mark was around, evenings used to be great fun because they both were masters at leg-pulling, though in contrasting style. Mark was large and loud, with a Yankee's penchant for drama and over-the-top debates. Chappell would be surgeon-like, using his words like a scalpel to make his point.

Most of the time, he was an original in such matters, but on one issue I can claim he was my follower. I remember a match in Colombo which WorldTel was broadcasting. It rained and rained that day, ruining any prospect of play.

Mark, who was in the box with us, turned to me and said, 'Looks a total washout; hard luck guys,' implying that there was to be no payment. My response to him was, 'Once the tie is worn and we are at the ground, the metre's running, Mark.' Chappell loved this so much that it became his standard dig at Mark whenever play looked doubtful.

Chappell has an elephant's memory. He remembers everything about everybody he has met, and particularly those he's played with or against. Over the past few decades, over several conversations, I've discovered his fascination for two players: Doug Walters and Erapalli Prasanna.

Walters he holds in high esteem for his skills and match-winning abilities; so much so that Chappell was willing to look the other way at some of Dougie's indiscretions. Prasanna he admired for his skill and mastery over flight, the ability to deceive the best batsmen in the air.

If you press the play button on these two players, Chappell
will spend at least a couple of hours on each.

He is a brilliant, incisive commentator because he's proactive,
and can read and analyse proceedings swiftly, more often than
not ahead of everyone else. But that's just one part of why he is
so admired among fans and the cricketing fraternity. The other
is his candour. He says it as he sees it, without beating around
the bush.

He may be wrong at times (though that hasn't happened
often), and never hesitates to correct himself. His passion and
love for cricket overrode all other affiliations and considerations.
When Greg Chappell asked Trevor Chappell to bowl underarm
against New Zealand, Ian Chappell was the biggest critic of his
brothers, especially Greg who was then captain.

I've always enjoyed Chappell's company. There are no false
starts with him. What you see is what you get. He is an excellent
storyteller who can have you in splits with his anecdotes and
impersonations. Whenever we toured Australia, my wife, Ritu,
and I would look forward to an evening or two with Chappell.
He always came armed with some bottles of fine wine and
new stories.

Outside of cricket, what you also get is a man who values
loyalty and friendship. He came to Bangalore for Mark
Mascarenhas's funeral. He needn't have. But then he wouldn't
be Ian Chappell.

BORN TO LEAD

Mansur Ali Khan Pataudi

Mansur Ali Khan 'Tiger' Pataudi was the biggest cricket star in India in the 1960s and 1970s when I was growing up. Boys would cut out his pictures from newspapers and magazines for their scrapbooks, and budding cricketers would wear their peak cap or floppy hat at a sharp angle like Pataudi did, without quite understanding why he wore it like that.

I heard a lot about Pataudi once I got into cricket as a schoolboy. He was the toast of the country, even when he had lost the captaincy in 1970-71 through a casting vote by then chairman of selectors Vijay Merchant. It was not just royal lineage which made him headline-worthy; he played with style and aplomb and abundant charisma ever since his debut in 1961-62. Because he was my all-time favourite Gundappa

Viswanath's first captain and mentor, I felt greater affinity, loyalty and respect for him.

When the West Indies toured India in 1974, the two most important players for me were Viswanath and Pataudi. In different ways, they made the series memorable. Viswanath was in perfect form, and Pataudi, having regained the captaincy, inspired a come-from-behind revival, which saw India level the series 2–2 after being 0–2 down. Though he didn't do much with the bat, Pataudi's influence on that series was enormous. Without his leadership, it was believed – and rightly so – that India would have got a hammering.

I watched the fifth and last Test of that series from the North Stand in Wankhede Stadium. To my dismay, Vishy failed to get a century by just 5 runs in the first innings, and, to my acute disappointment, Pataudi did not get too many in either innings and retired from the game. India lost the Test and the series, but won the respect of the cricket world for the manner of their fightback.

It wasn't until this series that I realized the handicap with which Pataudi had been playing throughout his career. My admiration for him grew by leaps and bounds, though the full import of what it meant to play with the sight in one eye virtually nil came much later, after I started playing international cricket myself. Even with normal eyesight, it takes a lot of practice, toil and adjustment to judge line and length correctly. How much more difficult must it have been for Pataudi? When you consider his achievements in that perspective, one can only marvel at what might have been had fate not intervened.

Many years later, on one of the tours to England, I was seated at the same dinner table as former England captain Brian Close.

Brian reeled off anecdotes of playing against Pataudi before he had lost his eye, and was emphatic that as a youngster, he was among the best in the world until his unfortunate accident.

I've heard a lot of stories about Pataudi – the man and captain – from those who played with or against him, like Vishy, Bishan Singh Bedi, Sunil Gavaskar, Anshuman Gaekwad, or those who knew him extremely well, like Yajurvindra 'Sunny' Singh and Ian Chappell. They have different and fascinating anecdotes and remembrances of the man, all converging finally to say that Pataudi was unique.

He had natural ball sense and grace, was a fine attacking batsman in his youth from all accounts and a brilliant fielder. Not just cricket, he excelled at squash, hockey and snooker too. He was born to play sports. But it was as a leader that Pataudi is best remembered.

Captains enjoy a lofty position in cricket, more so than in any other sport. But not all captains, for reasons of ability or personality, have lived up to this singular honour. On Pataudi, captaincy seemed to be a natural fit. He was only twenty-one when asked to lead the Indian team in a time of crisis. Nari Contractor, who was captaining the team, was hit on the head by Charlie Griffith in the 1962 series against West Indies and was ruled out of the Test. Pataudi's youth and inexperience had sceptics wondering how he would cope, but he showed he was to the manner born.

As captain, he had flair and charisma. Most of those who played with him for India aver he gave the team self-belief to compete overseas. He was also an out-of-the-box thinker. The all-spin attack which brought Indian cricket so many laurels in the 1960s and 1970s was conceived by him. I would even say he probably invented the forward short-leg position. Above all, he had a talent for recognizing and nurturing young players: Vishy, Ashok Mankad, Eknath Solkar and Gaekwad are just a few who benefited from Pataudi's mentorship.

I remember receiving an award from him somewhere as a youngster, but I got to know Pataudi personally much later. We did a lot of broadcast assignments together, and I gained a lot from his insights and how he read the game. He had a sharp and probing mind, which, combined with his vast experience, made him a formidable challenge for a fellow commentator to keep up with.

I enjoyed his company outside the box too. He was a man of few words, but whatever he said made so much sense. People thought he was aloof and snooty, but he was a very chilled-out person once the ice was broken, and a great storyteller with a wicked sense of humour. He could enliven an evening like few others I've met. Ritu and I struck up a good relationship with Pataudi and his charming wife, Rinku, and would visit them whenever we were in the capital. They were always a dazzlingly glamorous couple, but handled all the attention and fame with elegance and poise.

Though he kept himself out of administration, I thought Pataudi had a lot to offer Indian cricket, which had grown phenomenally over the decades and needed expert steering from those who knew and loved the game. When the Indian Premier League was launched in 2007, Pataudi and I – along with Gavaskar – were part of the Governing Council, and spent many evenings together, talking cricket, and often making it a point *not* to talk cricket, which was even more engaging because he was a man of such varied interests.

Alas, he left us too soon.

BANTER OFF THE BAT

Farokh Engineer

Farokh 'Dikro' Engineer was among the earliest pin-up boys of Indian cricket. In the 1960s, when cricket wasn't such a lucrative game and player endorsements were unheard of, Farokh appeared in the ad for Brylcreem, which ran in every newspaper and magazine. He couldn't go unnoticed even by those who had little interest in cricket.

As a youngster growing into the game, I was fascinated by the neat parting of his curly hair, and the big smile on his face in the advertisement. It spoke of confidence and success, and made me want to see my own photo in newspapers and magazines. In a way, Farokh became an inspiration for me to do well at cricket.

Whenever Farokh was on the field, batting or keeping wickets, the excitement among commentators on the radio was unmistakable. It was contagious. His exploits in the middle were dazzling. To my ten-year-old self, Farokh seemed a fantastic action hero, hitting fours, scoring at a scorching pace, taking diving catches and effecting lightning-quick stumpings. In the last Test of the 1972-73 series at Bombay, Farokh smashed 121. I didn't get to watch the match at Brabourne Stadium, but I did follow every ball of every match that India played through radio commentary.

When I finally saw Farokh play in person, however, it was a sore disappointment. India and West Indies were involved in a tantalizing series in 1974-75. The score stood tied at 2–2 when the final Test began in the newly built Wankhede Stadium. India had never won a series against the West Indies until then. I had a seat in the North Stand. The excitement among fans was sky high, as were the expectations. This time the sides looked evenly matched, but Clive Lloyd put paid to our hopes with a smashing double century. Two of my heroes, Gundappa Viswanath and Sunil Gavaskar, lived up to their reputations, but Farokh unfortunately got a pair, leaving me upset for days.

That was the last time Farokh played for India. The next I saw him was in England in 1980. I was captaining the Under-20 side. He called our manager, Chandu Borde, his India teammate of several years, and me over for a meal. Borde was his senior by a few years; I was his junior by a couple of generations at least. Yet, within minutes, Farokh had us both rolling on the floor with his jokes and wisecracks. He could bridge the gap in age and experience without any self-consciousness. Making friends with people, especially fellow cricketers, came naturally to him. In the forty years since, I haven't met a single cricketer who detests Farokh. Let me tell you, this is rare in the fraternity!

It was on the 1980 tour itself that I realized what a big name Farokh was in England. His personality, character and charisma had made him an international star. Perhaps just a whit behind Mansur Ali Khan 'Tiger' Pataudi. Apart from Tests, his fame came from his exploits while playing limited-overs cricket for Lancashire county along with Clive 'Supercat' Lloyd. These two were among the earliest professional cricketers in the English County Championships. They played together for seven or eight years, bringing in crowds with their dazzling batting and making Lancashire the most coveted team in the country.

Farokh left a tremendous impression on the county and its fans. Even today, if you go around Lancashire and talk about 'Rookie', everyone from ten to eighty knows him. His cricketing exploits are part of the county folklore. He helped them win two John Player League and four Gillette Cup titles, a big deal in the late 1960s and early 1970s. Later, he also became vice president of the county, so his association is deep and at several levels.

His success with Lancs should not obscure how good a cricketer Farokh was at the highest level. In 1967, in Madras, he racked up 94 runs before lunch against the West Indies bowling attack made up of Wes Hall, Charlie Griffith, Lance Gibbs, Gary Sobers and David Holford. Farokh was all guns blazing that first morning; one can only marvel at his talent and temerity.

Between 1970 and 1972, there were two series – one in England, the other in Australia, featuring the Rest of the World. Farokh was part of both these teams. This gives a clear idea of the esteem he was held in by the cricketing fraternity back then. Whenever I hear criticism about his wicketkeeping skills, I point this out, and there is silence. Speak to those who've played with him, and you'll realize how highly they all rate him. David Lloyd for instance would never cease telling me that Farokh grew in size every summer, but never dropped a catch. Beyond the joke, there was undeniable fact.

Farokh and I hit it off from the first time we met. We both went to the same school (Don Bosco), the same college (R.A. Podar), and of course, played the same sport. Above all else, we share a similar outlook on life: the one thing you have to be serious about is not be so serious that you miss out on the joys of life. With Farokh around, there is always banter and laughter. He sees the funny side of things, even when the joke's on him, a quality that I've seen in very few.

When we are together, I make it a point to speak to him in Hindi or Marathi. His responses are typically Parsi – in tone and accent, and liberally peppered with words that you are told as a child never to utter! Invariably, you'll see him with a plateful of food. He might be eighty-plus – though if you ask him he's likely to say just seventy – but he'll eat you under the table.

All told, Farokh is a terrific character and loved the world over. He's comfortable in any surrounding, adjusts and adapts quickly to people, food and what have you. A great salesman for the game as well as Indian cricket.

NIGHTMARE FOR BATSMEN

Dennis Lillee and Jeff Thomson

My father would often talk about Wes Hall and Charlie Griffith as the most fearsome bowling pair he'd seen. But growing up in cricket in the 1970s there was none deadlier than Lillee–Thomson. I wouldn't meet either till a decade or so later, but what made a huge impact on me was their devastating bowling in the 1974-75 Ashes series, which I followed closely on Radio Australia every morning before leaving for school.

How these two had the English batting shell-shocked became the subject of discussion among cricketing friends. Over the next few years, as the competition at the level I played in intensified, there were several young fast bowlers who fancied themselves a Dennis Lillee or a Jeff Thomson. I, too, was one of them, though I bowled left-handed.

Dennis Lillee is widely – and rightly – regarded as a 'coaching manual in action' for fast bowlers at any stage in their career. There is much to be learnt from watching his every step, from the run up and perfect side-on action, to delivery stride and follow-through that optimized effort and skill.

Lillee became role model, mentor and advisor to a galaxy of fast bowlers, including all-time greats like Imran Khan and Malcolm Marshall. He was the undisputed master of the nuances of swing and seam, control of line and length, change of pace, conserving stamina, etc., in his generation, if not the history of the game. This comes through clearly if you watch videos of his bowling throughout the 1970s, and particularly in the World Series Cricket when he was probably at the summit of his prowess.

He could have easily finished with 150 wickets or more had he not missed the seasons playing for the World Series, or had the wickets he had taken in the World Series been ratified as official. Some of the best batsmen of the time were in the World Series, and Lillee's clashes with Viv Richards for supremacy make for repeated viewing.

The bedrock of his success were his discipline and professionalism. Lillee raised fast bowling to the level of art, not just an expression of aggression. His work ethic was exemplary. The hours he spent in the nets were filled with purpose to get better and better.

Equally inspiring, if not more, was his comeback from a debilitating stress fracture in his lower back in his mid-twenties. Where most players would have given up on the game, Lillee saw it as a personal challenge to not just recover, but also become an even more dangerous bowler. His resilience in adversity, never-say-die attitude, and determination set benchmarks for the fast bowling community of his time and made him a hero to subsequent generations.

Lillee also played a big role in the pace revolution in India when he was associated with the MRF Pace Foundation as coach. The abundance of pace bowlers seen in India today can, in a way, be traced back to him. In spite of being a huge star, Lillee, in contrast to the highly demonstrative bowler he had been, showed rectitude right through, staying largely behind the scenes, and keeping his focus entirely on mentoring young fast bowlers. In this avatar too, he was the ultimate professional.

Batsmen who've played Jeff Thomson say that at his peak he was the fastest in the world, bowling at the speed of light! Even watching him from the safety of the dressing room would leave one trembling.

Among them were a few Indian batsmen who played against Thomson in the enthralling series Down Under in 1977-78, which resulted in a 3–2 win for Australia. Thomson took 21 wickets in the series. Not a mighty tally, but as my former teammate Anshuman Gaekwad told me, he was the only bowler the Indian team worried about through the rubber.

Thomson was consistently quick. With him, it wasn't controlled bowling, but all out aggression. To play him, apart from quick reflexes and sound technique, batsmen needed heart. Without courage, there was no way you could stand up to Thomson. As a precaution, it helped to fortify the medical kit too, for you never knew when he might get you with a nasty delivery!

What made Thomson different – and dangerous – was a slinging action, which gave batsmen no time to pick up length. Strength in shoulders meant he could extract steep bounce on any track – without pitching short. Especially on bouncy Australian tracks. Some West Indian batsmen who played him in the 1978 series at home recall his furious bowling, particularly a spell at Barbados when he had the likes of Viv Richards and Clive Lloyd hopping.

His partnership with Lillee is among the high points of Test cricket in the 1970s. When I was first introduced to Thomson, I wasn't sure what to expect. I had read so many intimidatory statements attributed to him that I was wary. But he turned out to be a chilled-out, fun character with a laconic sense of humour, a true boy from the country. I once asked him about his best figures in ODIs. 'One for twenty-one,' he said, which surprised me, till he added, poker-faced, 'four in hospital.'

Thankfully, I never had to play him.

SPIN MAESTROS

Erapalli Prasanna, Bishan Singh Bedi, Bhagwat
Chandrasekhar and Srinivasaraghavan Venkataraghavan

There has never been such an assemblage of high-quality
spinners in the same era at any other time in cricket history, and
their wondrous exploits are part of the game's folklore.

What this happy coincidence meant for Indian cricket is
reflected in the wickets Bishan Singh Bedi, Erapalli Prasanna,
Bhagwat Chandrasekhar and Srinivas Venkataraghavan took,
the matches they won and, no less significant, the impact they
had on fans and young players in the country.

At a personal level, I can say these four had an enormous
influence in shaping my career. By the time I was entering my
teens, I had more or less switched from trying to be a fast bowler
into a left-arm spinner. This was also the period when the spin
quartet was at its peak, inspiring budding cricketers and instilling
in them the confidence that slow bowling was a virtue.

As a youngster, I read every word written about them, and
never missed an opportunity to see them in action in Bombay,
either in domestic or international matches. Their success made

them household names and superstars not just in India, but wherever they played. There would be a buzz of excitement around the ground when Bedi, Pras or Venky was given the new ball after only a couple of overs, and the roar that greeted Chandra as he marked out his run up would have given Dennis Lillee or Malcolm Marshall a complex!

The four were completely dissimilar in build, bowling style and personality; even Pras and Venky, who were both off-spinners. This made their appeal stronger for fans, but life hellish for opposing batsmen. Bedi obviously commanded my attention more as a left-arm spinner, but the others were also equally charismatic. Then there was the ring of brilliant close-in fielders – Eknath Solkar, Syed Abid Ali, Ajit Wadekar, Yajurvindra Singh and Venky himself – all of whom became stars as these bowlers gave Indian spin a mythical dimension.

The credit for bringing these bowlers together and making spin India's weapon in international cricket goes to Tiger Pataudi. He assessed quickly and wisely that given the scant fast-bowling resources, India did not stand much of a chance against strong teams. By putting emphasis also on excellence in close-in fielding, Tiger came up with a match-winning formula. I can't recall a Test in the 1970s, either at home or away, when India did not play at least three spinners. In fact, in 1967 at Birmingham, Pataudi played all four of them!

I feel not enough credit is given to the spin quartet for India's success overseas. Records show that India's first away win came in New Zealand in 1968; we won the series 3–1, and spinners – Prasanna, Bedi and Bapu Nadkarni – contributed the most to India's success even on the green tops!

Among India's most memorable victories, the one against England at the Oval in 1971, came through Chandra, who flummoxed the English batsmen to claim 6–38. These spinners – in various combinations – were at the forefront of making the home series against West Indies in 1974-75 and the away tour against Australia in 1977-78 riveting.

These were the performances I grew up reading about, listening to on the radio or watching in person through the 1970s. By the time the decade ended, it was my privilege to know them personally. Venky even became a colleague in the Indian dressing room in 1983.

What made this spin quartet great?

Essentially, it was control over flight and the art of deception. This rolls easily off the tongue, but as any spinner will tell you, these are the two most difficult skills to acquire. Having played eighty Tests, I can vouch for this.

What made them special was that they were all attacking bowlers. If the trade-off was a few runs to lull the batsmen into error, they would go for it, rather than a few maiden overs. If the Indian outfield catching and ground fielding had been better, their averages would have been even more impressive.

Pras was a wily off-spinner with a vast repertoire of variations. The things he could do with the ball was amazing as I realized when we toured Australia in 1985 for the World Championship of Cricket. He was the team's manager, having retired from cricket six or seven years earlier. The midriff bore more kilos than in his prime, the back was not as flexible, but when Pras turned his arm over in the nets, he still got most batsmen out.

The delivery that went with the arm, with extra backspin, was deadly even then, but the big deception came from flight. What would look like a full-length delivery would suddenly dip, beating you for length. I am a tall man, but even I would be foxed by the trajectory and his variations.

Pras is a jovial sort. He kept us in good form, particularly during the World Championship of Cricket. Not just by his cheer, but also his deep knowledge of the game.

 Bedi was my bowling hero for obvious reasons. He's probably the best left-arm spinner ever. At least, I haven't seen anyone come even close in the past half-century. The languid approach and classical action was poetry. Like Pras, he was a master of flight, though being quite a bit taller, he didn't have to toss the ball as much in the air.

But Bedi had the ability to make the ball 'hang in the air' and wrong-foot batsmen. He also had a deadly arm ball that nipped many promising innings in the bud as the batsman failed to read the change in line and pace. His experiences in county cricket helped him a lot, especially in understanding the mindset of batsmen. This was my gain from playing for Glamorgan too, though I was hardly in the same league as him.

Bedi is a flamboyant, colourful character, hugely popular wherever he goes, and has the media eating out of his hand. He has a terrific sense of humour, with the ability to take a joke, which one sees in very few people. We've had our fair share of disagreements on cricketing matters, but nothing that couldn't be resolved over a glass of beer in the evening. I enjoyed his time as manager of the team in the early 1990s. In fact, he was instrumental in my playing as opener in England in 1990, one of my best tours.

There was no bigger match-winner than Chandra on his day. When on song, he could run through even the best batting line-ups. He was not just unorthodox, but unique. He turned a handicap – his polio-affected right hand – into an asset, leaving batsmen at sixes and sevens with his unusual action and the pace at which he bowled.

Syed Kirmani, technically the best I've seen behind the stumps, often told me that Chandra was the most difficult bowler to keep wickets to because of his arm speed, and especially when he bowled the googly, which would get extra bounce.

Chandra had retired from cricket by the time I joined the team, so I never got the opportunity to play with or against him. But I did meet him several times over the course of my nineteen-year career, as he was always at the stadium in Bangalore to watch matches. We struck up a good equation. He was a quiet, reticent man, but would come up with sharp analyses when you wanted.

Among the four, I got to know Venky's cricket skills, knowledge and personality first-hand because we shared the same dressing room on a difficult tour of the West Indies in 1983. He was the ultimate trier and a real fighter. He was thirty-eight then, but bowled beautifully against the great West Indies batting line-up of the time. Statistics do not reflect how well Venky bowled. He didn't have much luck with the numbers as our fielders came under pressure and quite a few catches of his bowling were put down. Kirmani missed a few off him, which got Venky all het up and he let the keeper have an earful. Then Venky dropped Gus Logie in the slips off my bowling, which prompted Kiri to tell Venky in an icy manner, 'It happens.' This didn't please Venky at all, who kept hissing under his breath.

He always loved a challenge, no matter the opponent. In the Barbados Test in 1983, Kapil asked me to open the bowling with him. Venky, who always fancied himself against left-handers, was itching to get at Lloyd. He asked Kapil through clenched teeth, 'Did I tell you I didn't want to bowl?' Kapil tossed him the ball soon after, and Venky dismissed Lloyd in three balls.

Had Pras not been around at the same time, Venky would have surely played more Tests. But what is not highlighted is his overall contribution to Indian cricket. He's been, at various stages, leading spinner, captain, manager, selector, and, for a long while, arguably the game's best umpire – making for a formidable body of work.

The 1970s in Indian cricket belonged to Sunil Gavaskar and Gundappa Viswanath, but also to this marvellous spin quartet. Batsmen tend to get more attention and glory in the game – particularly in India – but if one looks at performances that won matches in that era, the scales tilt towards these magnificent bowlers.

LEARNING IN THE BOX

Richie Benaud, Greg Chappell, Barry Richards, Tony Greig and Nasser Hussain

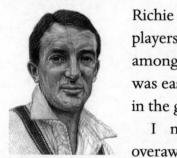

Richie Benaud was one of Australia's best players in the late 1950s and early 1960s, and among the finest captains. Post-retirement, he was easily the best-known TV commentator in the game.

I must confess to being somewhat overawed by him in my playing days. We met a few times when he was on duty in Australia for Channel 9, or the BBC in England when I was playing county cricket, but the conversations were brief largely because I was tongue-tied. Even then – not knowing that I would end up in the same vocation as Richie – I was impressed by the way he carried himself, the thoroughly professional approach he had to his job.

Not a hair was out of place, not a single crease on his shirt, and the pocket square in his jacket would be in perfect position when Richie faced the camera. He was always immaculately dressed. This was not so much out of vanity, as some thought, but from an acute understanding of the nature of the medium.

I learnt a great deal from him on how to be presentable on TV at all times. It tied into his credo that if you want to be a good pro, you better do the best job you can, starting with being a friend, not an enemy, of the camera, and through that to the audience you were reaching.

Television can be cruel. Even the slightest hint of shabbiness in one's attire, or a brief lapse in attention can be a major let-down. Benaud simply cut down the margin of error to virtually zero, becoming the best frontman for cricket shows and commentary in his time.

The other thing I learnt from him – though I must admit it was most difficult to emulate – was how to keep viewers engaged without bombarding them with excessive narrative. Richie understood better than most that TV is a visual medium. A great deal of the action doesn't need explaining. If anything, doing so diminishes the impact of the visual.

In the years that I got to know him personally, I realized he was a man of few words even when off air. But every word Richie uttered was of quality and significance. Sometimes his monosyllabic responses carried the gravitas of a full lecture!

His contribution to the game as broadcaster is formidable. His reading of the game, understanding which nuances to highlight, knowledge of players and their special skills was superb. His homework was always perfect. Richie was instrumental in paving the path for others to follow. He had a shrewd cricketing brain and his advice was always worth its weight in gold.

Greg Chappell was splendid with the bat. Tall and upright, with exceptional stroke play, he dominated bowlers all over the world in the 1970s. India was the only country he didn't play in (among ICC full members in his time), and I don't subscribe to the view that he would have struggled on our slower pitches. He scored a glut of runs in Pakistan where pitches are similar, and also in the West Indies where tracks can be spongy, unlike the even pace and bounce in Australia. His runs in England and New Zealand show not just how good Greg was against both swing and seam, but also how complete he was as a batsman.

Like all great batsmen, he had more time and stroke options at his command, even against the best bowlers. His batting was aristocratic, especially his ondrive, the full follow-through of the bat describing a beautiful arc. Natural ball sense made him a clever bowler, and he was perhaps the best all-round fielder of his time.

In the years during which I did commentary with Greg, I found him to be not only knowledgeable, but also ahead of the game. He was forward-thinking about where batting skills and technique were headed, what bowlers would have to do against batting improvisations in limited-overs cricket, the kind of temperament that optimized talent, etc. Often, while doing commentary somewhere, I would recall what Greg had said about some aspect of batting or bowling I was observing then maybe ten or twelve months earlier!

I always enjoyed picking his brain because he was so clear in his thoughts. Of course, asking his younger brother, Trevor, to bowl the underarm delivery in the final of the triangular ODI series against New Zealand in 1980-81 wasn't a great example of how to play the game, and this aberration has been like an albatross around his neck.

Greg is very different from his brother Ian Chappell. The latter is forthright at all times, whereas Greg tends to be reticent when he doesn't know the people around him. That said, he can be just as explosive as his brother when it comes to defending a point of view.

I was delighted when he became India's coach. I don't know exactly how things soured between him and Sourav Ganguly, but it is unfortunate that Greg's tenure became controversial and was brief, for he had all the credentials to make a big impact. What looked a win-win situation ended up sadly becoming a loss for both parties.

 Having watched footage of Barry Richards playing against the best assembly of fast bowlers the world has seen during the World Series Cricket, one could only marvel at how late he played even the quickest deliveries – with great results. And this towards the fag end of his career!

Barry could play only four Test matches before the curse of apartheid ended his Test career. Yet, in that brief period, he made 508 runs, which is fabulous. If this is not enough to establish him as the best batsman in the world in the early 1970s, his record in first-class cricket should push the verdict in that direction.

Playing in a match for South Australia against Western Australia in 1970-71, Barry got 325 runs in *a day* against the likes of Dennis Lillee, Graham McKenzie and Tony Lock. That must have been some knock!

One of the first books I read as a novice cricketer was *Barry Richards on Cricket: Attack to Win*. This and Gary Sobers's *Cricket Advance* went some way in shaping my fledgling career.

I met Barry when we were playing in Australia in 1991-92. He was then CEO of Queensland Cricket. We hit it off instantly, and when we both joined Mark Mascarenhas's broadcast team, the rapport became even better. When I began doing commentary alongside him, I understood what had made him such a great batsman. His grasp of batting technique, working out the angles which bowlers use on different pitches, among other nuances of the game, was an eye-opener for a fledgling commentator.

Much like Greg Chappell, Barry is a visionary in the art of batsmanship, but not restricted to just that. There is little he does not know about any aspect of the game: on the field, and off it, into administration, marketing, et al. I believe South African cricket could make far more use of his experience, knowledge and stature.

He's a fairly reserved man, and some serious family setbacks in the past decade have sadly made him withdraw from the game to a large extent. But Barry remains a steadfast friend, always ready with advice when I ask for it.

Nobody knew how to sell the game to audiences – anywhere in the world – better than Tony Greig. If cricket is where it is today, with scores of players making a decent livelihood even at the domestic level (at the international level, it's a different ball game!), Tony's role in this can't be undermined.

He was not only among the first players to join Kerry Packer, but also went about selling the concept of World Series Cricket to cricketers around the world. Some critics, including from within the fraternity, have called him a huckster, but I can't find even a few who didn't jump on to the bandwagon of commercialized cricket in the post-Kerry Packer era, in which Tony was a central figure. In that sense, he was ahead of his time, and looked at optimizing opportunities in and for cricket everywhere.

He was a bloody good cricketer too – let's not overlook that. A fine all-rounder and smart captain, he led England to a 3–1 win over India in 1976 for which he wasn't given enough credit. India was a strong team at the time with Sunil Gavaskar and Gundappa Viswanath to shore up the batting, and a galaxy of spinners to choose from.

Tony was extremely popular in India. He had a knack for understanding the sentiments and ethos of fans in different countries, and would tailor his commentary accordingly, as he did for Sri Lanka. We would discuss this often when the WorldTel commentary team met. In fact, this attribute of Tony's is something Mark Mascarenhas would highlight to me when I started out in the media. He became an iconic figure in Sri Lanka for the support he lent their cricket and its players.

From Tony, I learnt the importance of energy and voice modulation to make commentary enjoyable. Too often, former players who get into the media business live in a cocooned past. Tony was always looking to the future and made extra effort to reach out to fans proactively – and with great success.

Nasser Hussain is a fellow player and commentator with whom I've enjoyed sharing the mic. We've had our powwows – some on air too – but this has never affected the mutual respect we have for each other.

A few years my junior, Nasser had a distinguished career. There were many with better batting ability, but few were as doughty or committed. When the situation got tough, Nasser was at his best. Where he really excelled though was as captain. England had got into a pusillanimous phase in the mid-1990s and needed a capable leader with courage of conviction to pull them out of the rut. Nasser did this with strong control over players, self-belief, and imagination in exploiting his resources to the hilt.

As captain, Nasser was constantly seeking solutions and answers to prickly situations, which is what also makes him such a fine commentator. He is quick to spot trends in the passage of play, and his analyses are crisp, cogent and convincing. He reads the game superbly and has the words at his command to make a point without dithering.

What I like about Nasser is that while he does not mince words, he is never over the top. He has a lot of empathy for players and acknowledges that the vicissitudes of fortune can have a big impact in sport. This is a fine quality to possess – especially when, at times, cricket commentary feels like a circus show. Having played at the highest level for a number of years, Nasser sees cricket for the gloriously uncertain sport that it is.

FRIENDS

AND

RIVALS

CAPTAIN OF CAPTAINS

Clive Lloyd

Clive Lloyd's West Indies team of the 1970s and 1980s was a juggernaut, brooking no obstacle. India faced the brunt of their power in 1983-84, playing eleven Tests against them. Hand on heart, I can tell you that facing Lloyd and his band was an intimidating, unnerving experience. That Kapil Dev, Syed Kirmani and I were the only Indians who played all these matches tells you that the 'injured, unwell and out of form' list was long!

West Indies under Lloyd were fearsome, but also driven to excellence. Seven or eight members of that side, including the captain himself, would easily figure among the greatest players of all time. The teams Lloyd – and later, Vivian Richards – led dominated in all conditions and against all countries in batting, bowling and fielding. For almost fifteen years, they didn't lose a Test series anywhere, which is a fantastic record.

Lloyd's been accused of sullying cricket by relying on an all-pace attack. I heard this most when playing county cricket for Glamorgan, and there isn't anything more ridiculous. This was just sour grapes. England were royally hammered by West Indies under Lloyd for over a decade, and that obviously didn't go down well with many of their players, critics and aficionados. If I had the resources Lloyd had, I would have done the same thing. Any captain would.

The aim in cricket must be to win matches – within the rules of the game, of course – not live up to some putative ideal. If fast bowlers are good enough to win matches everywhere, the argument for including spinners becomes redundant. And vice-versa. In India, we've gone long years with three, occasionally even four, spinners because there was not enough bite in our pace bowling.

The theory of having a balanced attack is not unmerited, more so when you consider how the pitch and weather conditions can influence play. But what prevails over all other factors is what combination can help win the match. Rather than being criticized, Lloyd deserves credit for identifying a winning formula once he had assessed the talent he had at his disposal.

Having four or six fast bowlers is not as important as having the right quality of talent to win matches. In Andy Roberts, Michael Holding, Malcolm Marshall, Wayne Daniel, Colin Croft, Sylvester Clarke, Bernard Julien and Vanburn Holder, Lloyd found a rich supply of wicket-taking fast bowlers who could be deployed in all countries and conditions. The one thing which did help the West Indies, of course, was that the restriction on the number of bouncers per over came much later.

Having an abundance of talented players in itself does not make a champion side though, and this is where Lloyd's personality made the difference. He was a proud West Indian, had played enough county cricket to understand the value of professionalism, and he was a very good 'people's person'.

Spotting talented players, encouraging them, and binding them together as a team are the challenges confronting a captain. Oftentimes, this can be more important than strategy and tactical skills. Lloyd's strength was his ability to command respect from his players. He was like a father figure to them and moulded them into the formidable side they became – for which he deserves the highest praise. I watched from close quarters how he handled his players, knowing when to put an arm around someone who is struggling, what signals to send to someone who was being difficult that day. As a youngster on the international circuit in 1983-84, I imbibed some of his man-management skills which were of value to me later.

I have chosen to highlight Lloyd's captaincy because that is his enduring legacy. But even as a batsman, he was a champion. I saw him playing in person for the first time during the sixth Test at Wankhede Stadium in 1974-75. He smashed 242 not out, which not only pulverized the Indian bowling, but also gave me, a budding twelve-year-old cricketer, some sleepless nights.

Growing up, I read a lot about Lloyd's exploits: his sizzling stroke play and brilliant fielding, which earned him the admiration of teammates and opponents alike. One person who filled me in a lot about Lloyd – as a player and person – was Farokh Engineer, his Lancashire teammate of many years. I always loved to hear 'Rookie' Engineer talk about county cricket. He had some sumptuous stories of star players on the county circuit in which Lloyd featured quite frequently, so that by the time I met the West Indian legend, it felt as though I had known him for a long while.

Not that this stopped Lloyd from being ruthless on the field even with an admiring youngster. Cricket was serious business for him. By the time we met, he was in the sunset of a glorious career, yet a most dangerous adversary. On his day, even into his late thirties, he could wield the bat like a lumberjack. I haven't seen anybody hit the ball with as much power as Lloyd. In his younger days, I was told, the muscle in his strokes was even greater, which is frightening. Some of this is evident if you watch his brilliant 102 in the final of the 1975 World Cup, when he left even the Aussie fielders rooted to their spots with his shots.

He was not above some poker-faced gamesmanship on the field either. Often he would not give his decision to bat or field immediately after the toss. In those days, there was no mandatory interview post the toss. Lloyd would say he had to consult his team, go back to his dressing room, leaving the opposition guessing and sweating, and return soon after to say, more often than not, 'We'll field first.' It was just a tactic to put the other team under pressure.

Though he pursued success unrelentingly, Lloyd wasn't dour, grim and colourless. In fact, he had a great sense of humour with punchlines that would leave you rolling on the floor.

Lloyd's record as player is remarkable and as captain, extraordinary. Everybody believed in the stereotype of players from the Caribbean being happy-go-lucky. Clive Lloyd transformed them into ambitious, disciplined, hardworking world champions, the likes of which have not been seen before or since.

WRISTS OF STEEL

Gundappa Viswanath

In 1969, because of my parents' interest in cricket – particularly my mother, who knew everything about all the major players – I started out in the sport. The only source of following live matches then was the radio, and among the first cricketers, apart from Mansur Ali Khan 'Tiger' Pataudi, whose names got stuck in my head was Gundappa Viswanath, who made a century on debut against Australia in 1969-70.

Over the next few years, Viswanath turned from hero to idol. He hogged my imagination. Everything Vishy did on the field, I would unfailingly track through newspapers and the radio. In the early 1970s, once television came to Bombay, one could see him in action too and my admiration only grew. Listening to experts talk or reading what they wrote of Vishy's sizzling cuts and glorious ondrives was a terrific high.

Around this time, Clive Lloyd's West Indies team came on tour to India. Like most cricket lovers in the country, I was also consumed by this riveting series. Vishy was India's batting mainstay with a sparkling century at Eden Gardens followed by a blazing 97 not out on a fiery Madras pitch against Andy Roberts, Keith Boyce, Bernard Julien and Vanburn Holder. The series decider was played at Bombay, the first-ever at Wankhede Stadium, where I watched the action from the North Stand. Vishy missed a century (he made 95), much to my disappointment, but that did nothing to diminish my hero worship.

I would keep a scrapbook of sorts of Vishy's exploits and, whenever possible, if he was batting, keep my ears glued to the transistor. Among my most enjoyable memories growing up is following India's astonishing, record-breaking run chase at Port of Spain in 1976. Sunil Gavaskar and Vishy had by then become the crutches on which India's batting was supported. Get one early, the team would struggle; get both and it went kaput. Both batsmen were short of stature but mighty of deeds, and made us all feel proud.

After I got into competitive junior cricket, my biggest desire was to meet Gundappa Viswanath. In 1980-81, I was summoned to join the Indian team in New Zealand after Dilip Doshi got injured. Excited as I was to be chosen suddenly to represent India, I was nervous too. When I joined the team, Vishy put me at ease immediately. This instantly broke the barrier between a rookie and others in the team, including stars like Gavaskar and Kapil Dev. That won me over completely.

Watching Vishy from close quarters was obviously an even greater delight than from the stands or on the telly. He was an artist. He didn't build an innings, he painted one. The longer it lasted, the more beautiful and breathtaking it became. He had wrists of steel. When he played the square cut, the cracking sound of bat meeting ball would resonate around the stadium. Largely orthodox of technique, he would change this when playing fast bowlers, especially on bouncy tracks, getting beside rather than behind the line of the ball.

In the pre-helmet era, he was perhaps the best player of fast bowling in the world, because he could counter-attack effectively. Against the West Indies in 1974-75 and 1978-79, both times at Madras, he scored runs with aplomb on fast, bouncy pitches where most other batsmen failed. When I spoke to Clive Lloyd (captain in 1974-75) and Alvin Kallicharran (1978-79) a few years later, both said they hadn't seen better knocks on such pitches.

Vishy was not just supremely stylish but also India's best poor-wicket batsman; and the man the team would turn to in a crisis. That India never lost any Test match in which he scored a century highlights this. But he never hankered after personal glory, and averages meant little to him.

He was experiencing a lean period when England were touring India in the 1981-82 season. We had gone to see the Asiad Village coming up in Delhi. If memory serves me right, he didn't join us, choosing instead to remain in the bus. I went back and sat with him. Vishy looked a bit lost. He had been told by the selectors that this would be his last Test if he didn't score runs. What followed the next day was a masterful century at the Feroz Shah Kotla Ground, and a mammoth 222 at Chennai. The selectors went into hiding for a while after that!

I started my Test career as a tailender, and would pine to bat alongside Vishy. What seemed virtually impossible in 1981, became a reality in 1982 when I was asked to open at the Oval in the third Test between England and India as Gavaskar was injured and not playing. Vishy batted at number three and we put on a century partnership, which exposed me to his class, as batsman and man. The footwork, balance and swiftness with which he got into position to defend or play an attacking stroke was an unforgettable batting tutorial. During our partnership, Vishy also nursed me through some anxious moments against Bob Willis and Ian Botham. He didn't just offer words of comfort, but also insights, which went a long way in boosting my self-confidence.

Sadly, his career ended abruptly, after a string of low scores against Pakistan in 1982-83. Apart from Jimmy Amarnath and Sunil Gavaskar, no other batsman got enough runs in that series, so it was harsh that the axe should fall on Vishy. Actually, it was losing to Pakistan that was the problem. In a contest ruled more by sentiment than common sense, he became a scapegoat. I believe even now that Vishy had it in him to play a year or two more, and should certainly have been part of the tour to the West Indies where his experience and ability against fast bowling would have been invaluable.

Apart from his dazzling batsmanship, Vishy is also among the nicest human beings one can meet, unfussy and without tantrums – a humble soul wrapped in cricketing genius. He always played fair, irrespective of how others saw the game. He would walk, without waiting for the umpire's decision, if he knew he had nicked the ball. He didn't hesitate to recall Bob Taylor in the Jubilee Test when wrongly given out, though this cost India dearly.

If cricket is a gentleman's game, there is no better exemplar than Gundappa Viswanath.

GRIT AND GUMPTION

Mohinder Amarnath

Mohinder 'Jimmy' Amarnath was the gutsiest player I've played with or against. I can't think of another who took so many hard knocks – physically and otherwise – in a long career, but always came back with resolve and intent doubled. You could keep Jimmy out, but not down.

His bravado was understated. When we were touring the West Indies in 1983, he was hit on the mouth by Malcolm Marshall in one of the Tests. This would be a terrifying experience for most batsmen, even those sitting in the dressing room. Jimmy simply shrugged it off as one of those things that happen in sport. He was taken off on a stretcher, came back in an hour or so after receiving medical attention in the dressing room, and hooked the first ball he played for six! I don't think Clive Lloyd's mean machine, which had decimated rival teams, had seen any other batsman play with such force of character against their dreaded pace attack.

Jimmy's batting in the 1982-83 season was among the best overseas performances I've witnessed. He scored 500-plus Test runs in Pakistan and followed this up with 500-plus runs in the series in the West Indies. This, against the likes of Imran Khan, Sarfraz Nawaz, Malcolm Marshall, Andy Roberts and Michael Holding, among others. In that period, he was the world's best batsman against pace bowling. His ability to adjust from the swing and reverse swing of Imran and Co. in Pakistan to the hard pitches and predominantly seam and short-pitched bowling of the West Indies was remarkable and showed what an accomplished batsman Jimmy was and what India had missed by repeatedly picking and dropping him since his debut in 1969.

In a sense, we were kindred spirits, having started our careers as tailenders and playing in every position from number ten upwards, before establishing ourselves as top-order batsmen. The major point of difference between us, of course, was that Jimmy was a medium-pacer while I was a spinner.

Once he took up batting seriously, Jimmy bowled less and less, but was capable of surprising batsmen with his ability to coax swing and seam movement in his medium pace. In the 1983 World Cup, he shone as much with ball as bat, and won Man of the Match awards in the semi-final against England as well as the final against West Indies. Since he bowled so infrequently in the second half of his career, many batsmen did not know enough about Jimmy's skill with the ball and took him lightly, only to pay the price. In limited-overs cricket especially, he brought great value to the captain and the team by slipping in 5-6 overs of controlled bowling.

But it was as batsman that Jimmy made a big impact. This did not happen without huge commitment on his part. He spent hours and hours in the nets over months and years, working on his batting technique and skills to make the cut as a specialist. Yet, he struggled to keep his place in the national team as one or two failures would see him dropped from the side.

Although he was a giant in domestic cricket, scoring prolifically in almost every season and with a particular fondness for making runs against Bombay, his international career moved in fits and starts. He made his debut in 1969 against Australia, was dropped after one match, and didn't play a Test again till 1976. By this time, he had made the transition from being a bowling all-rounder to a specialist batsman who could also bowl and had a fruitful three years. But from 1979 to 1982-83, when he was included for the tour to Pakistan, he spent time in the wilderness. He had had his share of injuries, which also sullied his reputation, unfortunately.

Jimmy should certainly have played for India in 1981 and 1982, because he was in such excellent form in domestic cricket. Disappointing as these long years being out of favour must have been, he never lost heart. He was quite extraordinary in the way he worked on improving his batting, changing his stance, grip and approach to get better.

The helmet, newly introduced at the time, worked to Jimmy's advantage because he found the hook shot irresistible. But he also had a compact and tight defensive technique, which fast bowlers found difficult to penetrate. His batting skills weren't restricted to playing fast bowlers though. He was excellent against spin, using his feet splendidly. In the Tied Test against

Australia in 1986, he and Gavaskar set the tone for our run chase by taking the attack to Greg Matthews and Ray Bright.

Jimmy and I got along extremely well, often sharing a room when on tour. He was always chilled out, calm and unruffled, loved banter and singing Hindi film songs of which I knew little, but went along anyway. He was also very disciplined. In the days when fitness was not given the importance it is today, Jimmy set a benchmark for us.

More than anything else, I drew inspiration from his grit and gumption in how to handle difficult situations in the middle and off the field.

RUN MACHINE

Zaheer Abbas

 I used to call him Zaheer 'Ab-Bas', which roughly translates to 'enough is enough!'

Zed was a relentless run maker against India. In 1978, he scored 583 runs in just three Tests. In 1982-83, when we toured Pakistan again, he scored 650 runs in six innings spread over as many Tests. In 1984, on the tour that was truncated because of Prime Minister Indira Gandhi's assassination, he had made another match-saving century, perhaps as a reminder to himself that he had to make up for a poor series in India in 1979-80.

All told, Zed scored 1,740 runs against India in nineteen Tests at a whopping average of 87, which kind of explains why we were fed up of seeing him in the middle with bat in hand. He was a remorseless run getter.

When I first played against him, in 1982-83, he was in the best form of his life, spanking centuries at will and at a scorching pace too, sending fielders on a leather hunt in almost every match. Having been on the receiving end of this treatment a few times, I was relieved not to be playing in all the Tests!

At one venue, when we saw him park his car near our team bus, all of us groaned, 'Not here too!' Sure enough, he scored another century that day. Although that series is better known for Imran Khan's deadly bowling, it was the prolific run-getting of Zed (Javed Miandad and Mudassar Nazar too) that compounded our misery.

Nevertheless, I loved watching Zed bat. I think most of his opponents did – from the dressing room preferably, especially when he was taking bowlers to the cleaners in his inimitable style. The subcontinent is renowned for wristy batsmen – Mohammad Azharuddin, V.V.S. Laxman, Saleem Malik, among others – and Zed was one of the best.

Unless he was badly out of rhythm, even a cameo knock would compel attention. His stroke play was limpid and graceful. He wasn't a puny guy, but Zed hardly ever relied on power. He got runs with timing and placement, of which he was a maestro. He was a great judge of length, playing back or forward decisively. With a high backlift, he would come down on the ball late, flex his tensile wrists and give the ball a nudge in the direction he wanted. The timing was sweet, almost a caress, sending the ball speeding to the boundary.

Watching an artist exhibit his talent with finesse is always a source of great joy. Even his defensive shots led to runs because Zed had the uncanny and unerring ability to pick gaps. He was never into attrition, which meant that the only way to keep him quiet was to dismiss him early. Such wristy stroke play also means taking risks. Yet, the excellence of his technique and his temperament is evident from the numbers he notched up in Tests, county cricket and ODIs.

Zed scored over a hundred first-class centuries, more than fifty of which were for Gloucester. He also made a double hundred and a hundred in the same match *four* times. I didn't play against him in county cricket, and thank god for that! Three times against Somerset, he got a double and a century against an attack that included Ian Botham and Joel Garner. Viv Richards was in the Somerset team too, and I'm sure they have something to say about Zed's lust for runs.

Off the field, Zed is mild-mannered, friendly and always ready to help. Whenever I sought him out for advice, with my batting or on how to prepare for certain series, he came through unhesitatingly. Even outside of cricket, he would go out of his way if he could be of assistance. I remember having an issue with my visa in Pakistan once. One telephone call to him and it was sorted out. That's the lofty stature he enjoys in Pakistan: much as he does in cricket.

MY MENTOR

Sunil Gavaskar

Sunil Gavaskar was the best opening batsman I have seen bar none. I was his opening partner in quite a few Tests in the mid-1980s and, from 22 yards away, what you got was a sublime tutorial in batsmanship. Stance, grip, footwork, balance and stroke selection, judging singles and twos, running between wickets – he was perfection personified. He handled extreme pace with masterly technique and composure, showing no discomfort, providing relief and education to the batsman at the opposite end as well as those in the dressing room. Watching him bat, one got a clear idea of how the pitch was behaving, which bowler was in good form, who wasn't, and could structure their innings accordingly. It was both awe-inspiring and a delight to bat alongside him.

Interestingly, in the nets, Sunny could be a terrible batsman, often the worst amongst us. Journalists watching us at nets would write him off based on this, and be shocked when he came up with a brilliant knock in the match. He was not playing the fool during nets though. He used to draw up an agenda to work on some aspect of his batting, and once he was done, he would enjoy himself for the remaining time.

When I made my international debut, Sunny was the biggest star in Indian cricket. There was an unmistakable aura around him, off and on the field, and particularly in the dressing room. The way he built his 'mood' up for an innings or a match, and prepared himself – handling his kit, spending time by himself, reading a book or going through a set of rituals before he took the field – provided a big spike to my learning curve.

In so many ways, Sunny was my mentor. I was flown to New Zealand as an eighteen-year-old with meagre experience in domestic cricket. He had obviously not seen much of me, but the opinion of captains, especially if you are of Sunny Gavaskar's stature, are sought before any selection decision is made. The fact that he had agreed to my inclusion was a big deal for me.

In my first couple of years in international cricket, I watched Sunny intently, in the nets and in the middle, and started to take my own batting more seriously. I can't claim to have acquired even a fraction of the finesse and mastery of his batting, but I did become adept at was how to leave deliveries! This comes from an understanding of where your off stump is, and Sunny's judgement in this was without parallel. It proved a boon for me too as my batting career progressed, especially when opening the innings.

Sunny was also instrumental in my becoming an opener. The first time, ironically, was as his replacement. Fielding at silly point against England at the Oval in 1982, he was hit on the leg by a ferocious shot from Ian Botham and took no further part in the match. I had progressed from the number ten batting position in my first Test to number eight in this one and, in Sunny's absence, was asked to open the innings. It was tough, but I got 66. Though, I was back in the lower order immediately after, when he returned.

The following season, when we were being ravaged by Imran Khan and Sarfraz Nawaz in the six-Test series in Pakistan, Sunny came to me on the eve of the last Test at Karachi. His regular partners hadn't clicked. He said he wanted me to open with him. Although the webbing of my right palm was still healing from an earlier injury, sensing a challenge, possibly a long-term opportunity, and not the least for the privilege of batting along with him, I said yes.

Unfortunately, Sunny fell cheaply in the first innings. I went on to bat eight hours for 128, my maiden Test century. This was to be transformational in my career. It helped establish my credentials for a place in the top order. I played more regularly as opener after Sunny retired in 1987, but he was the biggest influence in my promotion as he had more faith in me than I had in myself!

As a batsman, Sunny was a master technician with a watertight defence. He could play all the strokes in the coaching manual with equal authority and poise. These virtues are usually good enough ensure a highly successful career for a batsman. What Sunny also had was a hard, combative mindset that refused to allow bowlers and rival teams even a blip of psychological advantage. This put him in the category of all-time greats.

There was nothing airy-fairy about his batting. If conditions were difficult, he would become even more particular about his stance, backlift, and follow-through of the bat to minimize risk. If conditions were good, he would ensure that the opportunity was not squandered, exploiting it to his own and the team's advantage by unsettling bowlers and the field with classical strokes. Any which way, his immense powers of concentration, capacity to bat flawlessly for long periods of time and insatiable appetite for runs came through.

Failures never fazed him because they were rare. What was even rarer was Sunny giving his wicket away cheaply. If he did get out for a poor score, he didn't get flustered. He would bury himself in a book, or listen to music. He didn't spend time brooding over it beyond what was necessary, knowing that he could sort out the problem in his head or in the nets. Even in the middle, when beaten, most batsmen rehearse the same stroke between deliveries to get it right the next time. Sunny didn't spend time on what had happened; instead, he settled down quickly to match wits with the bowler's next delivery. He had the amazing ability to switch off any negative thoughts or show weak body language that would give the bowler even a tiny advantage.

Added to all these attributes was physical courage. Fast bowling is a threat at all times, more so when you are opening the innings against the West Indies in the 1970s and 1980s. The mere thought of facing Andy Roberts, Michael Holding, Joel Garner and Malcolm Marshall would give batsmen nightmares and worse. (I know of a few whose bowel movements would go haywire, or who would sustain mysterious injuries on the eve of a match!) Sunny never flinched. Not against the battery of great West Indies fast bowlers, not against Imran, Sarfraz, Botham, Bob Willis, Richard Hadlee, Dennis Lillee, Leonard Pascoe, not any bowler. No other batsman in the history of the game perhaps has played so many exceptional fast bowlers with such a high degree of success.

Supreme technical excellence was a big factor in this, but absence of fear, I believe, was equally important. I remember batting with Sunny at Bourda (Guyana) in 1983, when a snorter from Macko reared up and crashed into his forehead (he was not wearing a helmet). Such was the impact of the blow that the ball rolled back to Macko in his follow-through. I was shaken and so too was Macko, though he tried to appear casual. But Sunny was genuinely unfazed even though he must have been in pain. He waved away my concern, settled into his stance, cover drove the next ball for four, and went on to make a superb century.

The West Indies fast bowlers, dreaded by batsmen the world over, were his favourites. He scored a whopping thirteen hundreds against them, including four in his debut series (Sunny's series aggregate of 774 runs in 1971 is still a record), and two in his last series against them in 1983-84 in India. The last two were vastly contrasting in approach. The century at Delhi in the second Test was stunningly aggressive. Sunny took on Macko, Roberts and Holding frontally, hooking, cutting and driving with a relish that caught fans, critics and certainly the opponents by surprise. This underscored how he had lived most of his career, in self-denial, because of the onus thrust on him to hold the batting together.

The double century at Madras took him past Don Bradman to his thirtieth century. This was a masterclass of a different kind. Sunny batted at number four in this match, but came in when the score was 0–2. It took him about a dozen deliveries to assess the pitch, and thereafter, he lorded over the proceedings, going on to score 236. I had a long partnership with him in this match, and his resolve to make a big score was apparent. We spoke very little while we were batting. He was never a great conversationalist in the middle except to caution his partner about how the pitch was playing, the tricks of a certain bowler or something new in the field placing.

He motivated himself by patting a spot on the pitch, no more. He put his head down for his first 20-odd runs and then became machine-like as he jogged past the milestones of 50, 100, 150 and 200 without blemish or sweat. Considering he had started the series with a 0 and 7 in the first Test, he finished on a spectacular high.

Sunny's belief in his own ability was of Himalayan proportions. Extreme professionalism and single-mindedness in achieving what he wanted kept him on top even in tough situations. Once he got his eye in, you could relax and put your feet up in the dressing room, knowing that he wouldn't return in a hurry. Even in domestic cricket, he was uncompromising in his quest for runs or supremacy against bowlers.

As is well known, he once batted left-handed against Karnataka in the Ranji Trophy semi-final in 1982. Some people thought he was taunting the rivals and gave him flak for it. But what Sunny wanted to do was nullify the threat from Raghuram Bhat on a turning pitch. He batted for almost two hours as a left-hander! Likewise, people were mistaken in believing that he didn't wear a helmet because of bravado. Actually, he just felt uncomfortable in one, but ask him today, and he'll say that he was wrong in taking such a big risk, even though he did all right!

At his core, Sunny was a fierce competitor and conscious of the fact that he was the best in the business. I remember him telling Geoffrey Boycott, who had gone past Gary Sobers's record run aggregate in 1981-82, 'Enjoy it for a year!' True to his word, Sunny sailed past Boycott within a short time. In the latter half of his career, Sunny was chasing his own records. When he reached thirty-four centuries and 10,000-plus runs, there was nobody in sight.

As captain, Sunny was shrewd and tough. He knew exactly what his team's strengths and weaknesses were. His Test captaincy record is modest simply because the bowling resources he had weren't good enough to win overseas, unlike now. But he led brilliantly in the 1985 World Championship of Cricket, getting the line-up of the team right by opening with Krishnamachari Srikkanth and me, Mohammad Azharuddin at number three, Dilip Vengsarkar at number four, and holding himself and Jimmy Amarnath back.

His cricketing persona could be intimidating. Playing for Bombay, Nirlons, and having teammates like Sandeep Patil, Karsan Ghavri and Dilip, who would lighten the atmosphere with their banter, made things a lot easier for me and other youngsters who joined these teams. But once he warmed up to you, Sunny was a very good friend and an excellent mentor.

Sunny and I have been associated with each other in some way or the other since 1981: in the Indian and Bombay dressing rooms, Sportsfield Society where we reside, and the commentary box. He's always had a mind of his own, and an acute understanding of his station in life. His contribution to Indian cricket is incalculable. He gave it spine and self-belief, and in doing so, became an inspiration for generations of batsmen. He still is one.

KAPTAAN KHAN

Imran Khan

Imran Khan is one of the greatest captains and players the game has seen. Why I hold this view hardly needs qualification. His record speaks for itself, and, if at all further validation is necessary, it comes from the experiences of those who played with or against him.

The first time I saw Imran play was on TV, when India toured Pakistan in 1978. He was then making a mark as one of the best all-rounders in cricket after a rather slow start to his career. His performances in Australia in the 1976 series and in Kerry Packer's World Series Cricket had helped his reputation soar. Against India Imran was quick, but without having quite the same control that would make him so formidable a couple of years later. His big hitting, especially in the exciting run chase in the third Test at Karachi, won him more renown in India then.

When Pakistan came to India the next season, I made sure to get a place in the North Stand at Wankhede Stadium. Theirs was a star-studded team, in which Imran was the biggest attention grabber – for cricketing reasons and otherwise. Imran didn't have a great match though, injuring himself and not bowling in the second innings. He struggled with his fitness through the series, which affected his team's chances. Pakistan lost the Bombay Test and subsequently the series against a determined Indian side.

But how brilliantly he made up for this disappointment when we toured Pakistan in 1982-83! By now, I was part of the Indian team and got to experience Imran's fantastic skills – with ball and bat – from just 22 yards away.

In his prime, in the early and mid-1980s, I'd unhesitatingly say he was the best fast bowler in the world. He had both pace and the ability to swing the ball lethally late. But for the injury he sustained in the series against us that prevented him from bowling for almost two years thereafter, he would easily have picked up 150–160 sticks more.

Imran's strength was his remarkable control over swing and reverse swing. The steeply curving late inswingers, or 'indippers' as they were called then, made life hellish for batsmen. We did not have much understanding of reverse swing then, and Imran had us bamboozled. His accuracy meant there was no respite. He could vary the length of the delivery depending on pitches, conditions and countries he was playing in. Even the best batsmen found it difficult to cope with the late movement that would send the ball darting in or away at the last second.

In the 1982-83 series, Imran demolished us – though we had a strong and experienced batting line-up – on pitches that did not really support fast bowling. Opening the innings in the sixth Test at Karachi in the series, I got to see Imran exhibit his full repertoire of marvellous skills. I scored my first Test century in that match, but there wasn't a single delivery when I was not under threat when he was bowling. Although Pakistan had already won the series and Imran was carrying a painful calf, his desire for success was unrelenting.

Over the next six or seven years, India and Pakistan engaged in several contests – Tests and ODIs – and Imran easily towered over all players in his side. This might be only perception, but he also seemed to be at his most aggressive against India. I realized what a fierce competitor he could be through a couple of exchanges in the middle.

In 1987, when I was leading the Under-25 team against Pakistan, Imran arrived late to the stadium for the match. He apologized, saying he was stuck in traffic. Fair enough, but he wanted to start bowling straight away, which I wasn't agreeable to as this was against the rules. Sensing the umpires were vacillating, I told them to mind their own business and go by the book. Imran's message to Wasim Akram and the other bowlers in that game was to bounce the shit out of me.

Sometime later, when we were playing Pakistan in Sharjah, I suddenly got stomach cramps while batting and requested for a runner. Imran refused. We were 100 something for no loss then. I fell in a couple of deliveries. From a solid start, wickets started tumbling and we went on to lose the game chasing a modest 240-odd.

Imran had not forgotten what I'd done to him earlier and paid back in kind. But while he played it real hard, he left the contest on the field. Off it, he was friendly but reserved, keeping pretty much to himself. Many thought him to be aloof and snobbish; I think he was reserved, and not one to socialize readily.

Among the four great all-rounders of that era, Imran was the best batsman, technically and temperamentally. He could bat at any number and, more importantly, according to what the situation demanded. His long stint in county cricket and experience in the World Series Cricket had made him value professionalism over pointless bravado. Wasim Akram told me about the countless lectures, some of them very stern, he and other young players got from Imran if they had thrown their wicket away or bowled poorly even though Pakistan had won.

Winning the World Cup at the fag end of his career, when he was a quarter of the bowler he used to be, was nothing short of extraordinary. It was sheer self-belief that goaded Imran to chase this honour. He led from the front, batting up the order in the semi-final and final to control the innings.

The pride that he took in playing for Pakistan not only boosted his own performances, but also inspired several generations of young cricketers in his country to excel. He was a demanding captain, but also made heroes of others, his greatest quality as a leader. He was autocratic but also inspirational, and determined to leave behind a legacy.

I admired his poise and calm demeanour on the field. He never appeared ruffled, however grave the situation; never gave opponents an inkling that he was under pressure. His decision-making was swift, and, if it didn't work, he moved on, trying the next gambit. He was a man of action, not a brooder.

Also of unwavering resolve. The cancer hospital Imran built in memory of his mother is testimony to this. It took years to raise funds and see the project through, but he never let up.

Soon after retiring, he joined politics, making little headway in the first few years. When I asked Wasim Akram on one of our commentary assignments whether Imran had made a mistake by jumping into politics, he replied, 'If Khan sa'ab has decided on something, he will never give up, even if he is a hundred years old.'

A decade later, and more than twenty years after entering politics, Imran Khan became prime minister of Pakistan.

MR PERFECTION

Richard Hadlee

I have very fond memories of Richard Hadlee. In my debut Test series against New Zealand (1980-81), I took 15 wickets and was rewarded with a pair of shoes from the great man himself. I don't know what prompted him to do this, for he didn't inquire about the size of my feet. But the shoes fit me perfectly.

For a starry-eyed nineteen-year-old only recently initiated into international cricket, this was a huge honour. As a bonus, the shoes carried his signature too. As I realized soon, in those days, everything to do with cricket in New Zealand was autographed by Hadlee, that's how popular he was!

I'd say Hadlee's had the biggest influence on New Zealand cricket. Martin Crowe, who played in the same era, came close, and Kane Williamson, master batsman and a fine captain, may surpass both in the future. But till date, Hadlee reigns supreme.

In a country where cricket trails behind rugby and some other disciplines, Hadlee's exploits made him a national hero, inspiring countless youngsters as he won several matches almost single-handedly, often against stronger opponents.

In 1985, more than a decade after coming into international cricket, he demolished Australia with 33 wickets in just three Tests. Trans-Tasman rivalry is bitter, and Australia have enjoyed the upper hand on more occasions, but, in that series, they were blown away by Hadlee, by now thirty-five, but still hungry for success, bowling with stamina and skill.

Even in conditions unsuited to fast bowling, Hadlee, at the peak of his prowess, could be unplayable. When New Zealand toured India in 1988, we knew he was the main threat to our batting, but we had no inkling what agony he would cause. He got 18 wickets in that series, tormenting our top order in every match with his masterly use of the ball – new and old. In the second Test at Mumbai, he got 10 wickets on a Wankhede slow turner where many renowned fast bowlers had been brought to their knees. Of the 40 wickets in that Test, fast bowlers got 17, of which Hadlee got 10!

The discussion in our dressing room during that series centred on how to see off Hadlee's opening spell. Easier said than done. He almost always claimed a wicket in his first few overs. In fact, if the odds were good, I'd bet on him to take a wicket in his very first over anywhere in the world!

It's impossible to highlight one attribute as Hadlee's main strength. Control over movement, swing or seam, and pinpoint accuracy were what set him apart. Although he got barely a few inches' deviation, especially in the subcontinent, it was enough because he gave batsmen little leeway with his immaculate line and length.

In his best years during the 1980s, when he was picking up wickets prolifically in New Zealand, India, England, Australia – everywhere in the cricket world, in fact – Hadlee bowled fast-medium. The rigours of county cricket had forced him to compromise on pace to survive in the game. But on his day, he could be as quick as anyone. He modelled himself on Dennis Lillee in this and several other respects, where skill enhancement and a lengthy career were concerned. His other similarity with Lillee was in the way he appealed, full-throated, almost intimidating the umpire. But, unlike Lillee, Hadlee was not a confrontationist.

Criticism against him – even within the New Zealand team, as the buzz went – was that he was self-centred. My own experiences with him suggest Hadlee was intent on self-improvement, which he believed would help the team.

I spent a lot of time with Hadlee on the county circuit. He was a senior pro, having spent a number of years playing for Nottinghamshire. Along with Clive Rice, Hadlee formed one of the most feared pace attacks on the circuit, especially on the greentops at Trent Bridge, where these two wreaked havoc for several seasons. His rich experience was invaluable, his knowledge deep and he never held back on advice. I would constantly pick his brains on how to utilize county experience for improving at the international level.

Where cricket was concerned, Hadlee lived in a universe all his own. Like Sunil Gavaskar, he could cut himself off from all distractions when in the middle and go about his task with ruthless single-mindedness. There was no wasting energy or effort; even his net sessions were intense.

He was not a mean batsman; he could tonk the ball hard over long distances which opponents would disregard at their own peril. But because he chose to focus so much on bowling, his batting suffered somewhat.

Amongst the four great all-rounders of the 1980s (Ian Botham, Imran Khan and Kapil Dev being the others), I rate Hadlee as the best bowler for sustained hostility and wicket-taking ability in a long career. In sheer control, skills and willpower, he was peerless.

THE KING

Vivian Richards

Vivian Richards was simply the best batsman I've played against or seen. In the last half-century at least, no one has dominated the bowling quite like him. With or without helmet, he was a master blaster in the truest sense of the term.

Some young sceptics question his greatness, saying he scored just over 8,000 runs and averaged a shade over 50, when quite a number of batsmen from the modern era have achieved better stats. But this overlooks the fact that Richards scored over 3,000 runs in the World Series Cricket at an average of over 60 against bowlers like Dennis Lillee, Len Pascoe, Max Walker, Imran Khan, Mike Procter and Clive Rice. For the doubters, I'd recommend they watch the World Series Cricket on some OTT platform. They'll be instant converts to Richards greatness.

Stats in any case, are only an index to a cricketer's greatness, not necessarily complete validation – unless one is talking of Don Bradman or Gary Sobers. A player's true worth is assessed from the number of matches his personal contribution helped win. In this respect, Richards stands head and shoulders above any other batsman in the past fifty-odd years.

The number of times he got hundreds in finals – international and domestic – remains unmatched. He enjoyed the spotlight and the big occasion brought out the best in him. But while he loved an audience, Richards wasn't a show pony, rather a thoroughbred professional, who understood the expectations reposed in him and played to meet these. His century in the final of the 1979 World Cup is arguably the best in the history of the tournament for the manner in which he demolished the English bowling.

He looked to be in an even more murderous mood against us in the 1983 World Cup final, smashing the bowling to all parts of Lord's. Fortunately, he miscued a pull stroke off Madan Lal and Kapil Dev took a stunning catch to dismiss him. Richards would have otherwise run away with the match had he batted a few overs more. This was the turning point of not just the match, but of Indian cricket history.

Richards had both substance and style. Complementing his supreme talent was a swagger that made him the centre of attraction in whatever he did on the field. He exuded immense self-confidence, the likes of which I've never seen before or since. Growing up on the beaches of Antigua, swimming, running, playing football and cricket, had made him naturally strong and physically intimidating. Along with a keen eye and fantastic reflexes, he used his physical strength to great effect. He would play the ball very late, the point of contact most often under his eye, so he was always in the right position and could play the stroke where he wanted, not where the copybook dictated. That was his brilliance, not a limitation, and explains the huge success he enjoyed in England and on the turning pitches in India.

He was easily the best hooker and puller I've seen, reading length quickly and getting into the correct position with twinkling footwork to send the ball to the fence or over. Against slow bowlers, he would use the depth of the crease to play the cut or pull the ball. An extremely tough competitor, he had a great desire to succeed at all times and never yielded an inch.

Playing against England, especially, brought out the best in him. Theories that he would be vulnerable against late swing or spin in bowler-friendly conditions because he seemed to play across the line were all poppycock. These were to do with technical orthodoxy, which players from the Caribbean, many from the subcontinent, and even several Aussies, have shown to be limiting rather than beneficial.

Richards had the ability to spoil a good game of cricket for the opponents with his genius. In the first Test against us at Kingston in 1983, he smashed 61 off just 36 balls, hitting five boundaries and four sixes in a whirlwind knock which helped West Indies win a match that had looked doomed to be a draw.

Then there was the century he hit at New Delhi in 1987. It was a turning track, and we had really fancied our chances, but he quashed all such hopes with a counter-attack that was as brutal as it was brave. It was this ability – to turn things around dramatically within a short time – that made Richards so dangerous and special.

His overly aggressive demeanour didn't mean he was a slam-bang batsman. He naturally preferred attacking to defence, but he could alter his approach if the situation demanded. In the Madras Test in 1988, which I captained as Dilip Vengsarkar was injured, Richards batted for over four hours in making a half-century. I tried to rile him with some pointed banter, hoping to get him out and finish the match early, but Richards wouldn't take the bait. He just kept chewing gum, and glared back at me and the close-in fielders who were trying to make him lose his cool. His stony silence and smouldering eyes seemed to say, 'Watch it next time, guys, I'm going to get you.' When we toured the West Indies a year later, he did.

From the time he scored 829 runs in seven innings against England in 1976, Richards became the game's biggest drawcard. He brought bums on seats wherever the West Indies played. Devastating stroke play was his calling card, but he was also a livewire in the field and a brilliant catcher. In a side that had so many stars, Richards stood out.

On the field, one didn't get any favours from him. That's how it should be in professional sport at the highest level. We were in the same team for Glamorgan for two years, and I really looked forward to playing with him. Unfortunately, he was injured both seasons.

Off the field, he is a terrific guy, loves pranks and didn't put on any airs about being a superstar. I can say he's a good friend of mine. Over the years, we've met several times, shared a lot of old memories and spoken about new stuff to look forward to. He still looks as fit as he did in his pomp when he was 'King' Richards, proudly wearing the West Indies cap.

POWER AND PANACHE

Gordon Greenidge

 When you talk about the West Indies team of the 1980s, the names that come readily to mind are Clive Lloyd, the battery of pace bowlers and the redoubtable Viv Richards. Gordon Greenidge is hardly mentioned in the same breath, which is unfair to the talent he possessed and his immense contribution to West Indies cricket, especially in making the 1980s side possibly the greatest in the history of the sport.

Greenidge was a fantastic opening batsman, as aggressive as any that have come from the great Caribbean lineage. He could hit the ball with brutal power. His square cut, legendary as it was, was only one among a vast array of strokes that singed cricket grounds everywhere.

The difference between Greenidge and all the other great West Indian batsmen is that his technique was orthodox, almost

English, if you will. This was in part because he spent his
formative years in England, learnt all his cricket in a system that
put getting behind the line of the ball, et al., as sacrosanct. But
this did not limit Greenidge's inborn Caribbean flair. In fact, a
strong grounding in technique made him even more formidable.

Because his defence was so sound, and because he could also
switch into attack mode with aplomb, Greenidge could bat in
multiple gears, which compounded the problem for bowlers.
He was comfortable on the front foot and back, against swing,
seam, the short stuff, and spin. I always found him a very
difficult batsman to bowl to as he wouldn't allow me to settle
into a length.

Greenidge's opening partnership with Desmond Haynes
broke records – and the resolve – of many opponents. Their
understanding in the middle was superb, especially when
running between wickets. And if they both settled in, which
was often, spectators would be treated to a magnificent – albeit
painful for bowlers – jugalbandi of strokes.

Greenidge could be destructive on his own. One series
I followed closely was West Indies's tour of England in 1984.
I was only a few years old in international cricket. The West
Indies were such a dominant side (despite losing the 1983 World
Cup final just months ago) that I would track them diligently to
understand what made them tick, and if there were chinks that
could be exploited.

The second Test at Lord's was turning out to be a close affair.
In fact, West Indies looked under pressure to survive the last
day in swinging conditions against Ian Botham, Bob Willis and
Neil Foster. Having made 245 in the first innings, it seemed

improbable that they would get the 342 target David Gower had set.

In a stunning display, Greenidge scored 214 to help West Indies win. Only one wicket fell as the runs came at more than 5 an over. He batted with the power of a lumberjack, leaving England battered and bruised. It remains among the most astonishing knocks in the history of cricket, and I'd strongly recommend those who haven't seen it yet to watch it on YouTube or some other archive. It will also highlight the skills that made Greenidge so feared by bowlers all over.

Greenidge scored heavily against us in the 1980s. The swift adjustments he made from Caribbean pitches to those in India was proof of his ability to read surfaces as well as his skill against spin. Viv Richards was the megastar, but Greenidge was no also-ran. In fact, we spent as much time strategizing to get him out as we did for Viv, but our success rate was hardly enviable.

There is, of course, that one time during the 1983 World Cup final when we got him out cheaply – among the most memorable moments in Indian cricket history. Greenidge misjudged Balwinder Sandhu's steep inswinger and was bowled shouldering arms. Viv Richards's dismissal is considered the turning point of the match, but getting Greenidge so early was hugely significant too.

A solid, all-conditions opening batsman who scored runs across the world and would set up matches for his side. I'd club him with Sunil Gavaskar, Virender Sehwag, Geoff Boycott and Graham Gooch as the best openers in the last half-century.

GLUTTON FOR RUNS

Graham Gooch

In the summer of 1990, the India team reached Lord's for the first Test in high spirits; having won the two ODIs preceding the series, our batsmen and bowlers were looking in good form.

It had been a warm English summer till the time we reached Lord's. The grey clouds looming overhead during toss on the first morning of the match hinted that the weather might be turning. This prompted captain Mohammad Azharuddin – with, admittedly, some prodding from me – to bowl first if he called correctly.

He did, and we asked England to bat. Mike Atherton and Graham Gooch came out to open the batting. We got Atherton cheaply. Gooch had moved steadily to 33 when he was dropped behind the wickets. This was the decisive moment of the match, perhaps the series. If Gooch had fallen, the pressure on England would have been enormous, with conditions still helpful for fast bowling. Instead, the grey skies cleared and we spent the next two days on a leather hunt, Gooch giving us the kind of drubbing, the memory of which still gives me aches. He played every stroke you can think of as we threw our all at him and went on to score 333, showing our bowlers and fielders every inch of the Lord's ground.

This was a match in which quite a few hundreds were scored, including one by yours truly, but Gooch overshadowed everyone. After his triple hundred, he scored 123 in the second innings, combining an insatiable hunger for runs with furious hitting, which enabled England to declare in time and force a result. In the series, he scored a whopping 752 runs, the second-highest aggregate for any captain in one series, the first being Don Bradman with 810 against England in 1936-37 as I gather from my statistician friends. Gooch's runs, however, came in only three Tests, The Don's in five, which should establish how dominant the former was in 1990.

Gooch had a penchant for scoring runs against India, much like Zaheer Abbas (both also scored more than 100 first-class centuries!), and the most painful of these came during the semi-final of the 1987 World Cup at Wankhede Stadium.

We were favourites to win this match after a string of impressive performances, but Gooch swept us out of the final with a remarkable century.

In the post-mortems that followed the match, the Indian spinners were widely criticized for bowling the wrong line to Gooch. This is unfair to Gooch for it dismisses his stellar preparation. Looking back over three decades to that innings, Gooch had played the sweep with immaculate positioning and timing, frequently picking us spinners from off and middle. As any overseas batsmen will attest, this is hazardous on Indian pitches. But that day, this was the secret to Gooch's genius.

I always found it difficult to bowl to Gooch because of his stance, with bat held aloft. He was a tall man, swift on his feet, and would swoop down on even a minor lapse in length. The question of what the right length to bowl to him was worried not just me but other spinners too.

Gooch was not only a fantastic player of spin, but of pace as well, more often than not taking the attack to the bowlers on even hostile pitches. His performances against Australia, West Indies and Pakistan – who boasted the best fast bowlers in that era – are hugely impressive. He had lovely drives in front of the wicket, could hook and pull with aplomb, and was a fine reader of late swing, making the task of fast bowlers that much harder. To score the number of runs he did against the dreaded West Indies pace attack in their prime, with that bat-high-in-the-air stance, shows how quick his reactions were.

Some batsmen have higher batting averages because of the number of not outs. Gooch's figures might appear modest in comparison, even though he was way ahead in performances, only because he has fewer unbeaten knocks. His hunger for runs was amazing, as I saw in county cricket where he made runs day after day, season after season, with machine-like regularity. He and Allan Border held up the Essex batting for quite a few years, and I must confess that this was one contest I did not quite look forward to when playing for Glamorgan.

Success did not come to Gooch on a platter. He worked harder than most for it, and was extremely demanding of fellow players to show similar commitment. This is perhaps why he wasn't the most popular guy in his own dressing room when he was captain.

I'd say unhesitatingly that he was England's best batsman in my time. To start with a pair on debut and finish as England's highest run getter (till Alastair Cook overtook him), despite missing three years for going on a rebel tour to South Africa, is a stupendous achievement.

IN THE FAST LANE

Michael Holding, Andy Roberts and Joel Garner

In the 1970s and 1980s, the West Indies were the best side in the world primarily because they had the most destructive pace attack in the history of cricket. Clive Lloyd masterminded the change in approach when he dumped spin and pushed for fast bowling as the recipe for success.

It worked, not only because the tactic was brilliant, but because the supply of fast-bowling talent was of supreme quality and, perhaps even more importantly, unending. The problem for batsmen wasn't to survive one or two superb fast bowlers, but an assembly line of them.

If the regulars were ill or injured, those who replaced them were equally good and lethal. Colin Croft, Sylvester Clarke, Patrick Patterson, Wayne Daniel and Winston Benjamin would have been long-term frontline bowlers in any other cricketing country. Their opportunities to represent the West Indies were limited because Malcolm Marshall, Andy Roberts, Mike Holding and Joel Garner firmed up their places in the side early, kept getting better and couldn't be dislodged.

When this era lapsed, the baton was passed on to Courtney Walsh and Curtly Ambrose, who were no less deadly than their predecessors. West Indies cricket hasn't been the same since Walsh and Ambrose retired.

I firmly believe that Malcolm Marshall was the deadliest and best fast bowler I've faced or seen. But the others were only marginally behind. What was fascinating was how different they were from each other.

Michael Holding was pure joy to watch, but not to face. He could be lightning quick, with short-pitched deliveries that flew like missiles past your throat, nose or head. He had a deep stare too if you played and missed; no words, just a mean, hard glare, the message of which was hardly in doubt.

Holding was a quarter-miler in his formative years, and had he not chosen cricket, he may have made the cut, representing Jamaica at the international level in athletics. He was tall, lithe and aesthetic; a Rolls Royce among fast bowlers, barely making a sound, and would have spectators transfixed with his athleticism. When he came in off his full run up, it was a sight to behold.

After he sent down a delivery, the crowd would break into a buzz, discussing and debating what had happened, what would come next. This was especially true when he played in Jamaica, where he was obviously adored.

I'll never forget on my first tour in 1983 when Holding came off his full run up in front of a packed Sabina Park in Kingston and sent Sunil Gavaskar's leg stump cartwheeling almost all the way to Joel Garner at fine leg. It was an extraordinary sight and the stadium simply exploded.

In the West Indies, Holding bowled off his full run up, but when he came to India after the World Cup, he cut down on his pace and run up, conserving his energy on the slower pitches. But he was no less dangerous for this; if anything, he was more accurate, and bowled more unplayable deliveries.

After retiring, Holding took up the mike (if I may be permitted a pun), and has enthralled viewers with his astute, candid observations delivered in the delectable Caribbean accent. He is among my closest friends on the circuit, and someone from whom I keep learning constantly, about the game, commentating and life.

Andy Roberts was the most skilful of the West Indies fast bowlers I played. He would always have batsmen wondering what he was going to do next. He was inscrutable, hardly spoke in the middle, and his body language gave little away. When he was on song, batsmen had to rely on instinct and luck against him. His most dangerous delivery was the bouncer, because he had two kinds, varying in pace, length and line. If a batsman pulled or hooked him, he would be fending off the 'other' bouncer next to save his head, or get dismissed trying to hook from an awkward position.

I understand Roberts was even more lethal in the 1976 series against India. By 1983, he was ageing, almost a decade of county cricket also having taken its toll. But he had become craftier, and Lloyd would invariably turn to him for a breakthrough. He took 25 wickets when we toured the Caribbean in 1983, which shows how good he was even in his sunset years.

Joel Garner, touching the sky at 6'8" in his shoes, did not have the pace of Macko, Holding or Roberts, but he could coax bounce out of any pitch, which made him lethal. And he had perhaps the deadliest yorker in his time, as the 1979 World Cup final showed.

At his pace, he had to have immaculate control to be effective, and Garner had this amply. He gave very little scope to batsmen to score singles, let alone boundaries, bowling a good length or just short for extra bounce. It was Garner's parsimonious bowling as foil to Macko, Holding and Roberts that made the West Indies bowling in the 1980s so successful. All escape routes were sealed. A glance at the averages of these bowlers and no further explanation is necessary. There was just no respite for batsmen!

READY FOR BATTLE

Javed Miandad

Javed Miandad was a street fighter, and I don't mean that derisively. He was sharp, cunning, audacious, and possessed a never-say-die spirit that kept him in good stead both on and off the field.

Looking back, Miandad comes across as an even more multi-faceted and fascinating batsman. He was an opportunist on the field, who relied on sharp instinct as well as a smart reading of the situation, conditions and opponents, but he was also a big-innings, big-occasion player. He could use patience and stealth to win a battle in the middle, or be in outright attack mode, playing strong, improvised strokes and using aggressive body language to intimidate opponents. He had enormous belief in his own abilities and was not shy of sledging a bowler, however mighty their reputation.

In fact, in psychological one-upmanship, there was no one better than Miandad in my time. His greatness lay in his unique combination of bluff and bluster with hardcore batting skills. His unorthodox technique did not make him a pretty sight, but certainly made life hell for bowlers, for he had an answer to almost everything that was thrown at him. Quicksilver footwork, a keen eye and a rare ability to make last second adjustments in defence or offence by shifting his grip on the bat left many a bowler wringing his hands in hapless frustration.

In his heyday, Miandad was an athlete and a half. While most people remember him for his batting average, the number of runs and centuries he scored, for me the most abiding memory is his running between the wickets: he was the quickest I've seen over 22 yards. He could spot runs where presumably none existed, and would pounce hawklike on even the slightest tardiness or lapse by a fielder. It was as if he had eyes in the back of his head!

The capacity to convert ones into twos and twos into threes made him even more dangerous when he was with tailenders. He was brilliant at marshalling the strike and drove fielding teams to despair. Much like his former captain Asif Iqbal. The two made the best pair I've seen where running between the wickets is concerned.

I had yet to play international cricket when India toured Pakistan in 1978, but that series had everybody in the subcontinent pay attention. There were outstanding performances from both teams, but what had everyone in thrall was the way Asif and Miandad ran between the wickets to set up victory in the third Test at Karachi. It was simply unbelievable and, I dare say, made India's cricketers focus more on this aspect.

Miandad's innings against India in the Austral-Asia Cup final in Sharjah (1986) where his last-ball 6 got Pakistan an incredible victory and everlasting fame for himself is still among the three greatest ODI knocks I have seen. It was brilliant in concept and execution. A tour de force.

When the top-order batsmen and all-rounders had fallen, we were sure Pakistan would lose the match. All Miandad was doing was picking up runs in singles, twos and sometimes threes, almost giving the impression that he too didn't believe victory was possible. That was very clever deception for he kept his team in the hunt by hogging the strike, and not allowing us to get at the tail. It was only when the target was within striking distance that he started taking calculated risks.

It was a masterclass demonstration on how to put up a match-winning performance under pressure. Almost three-fourths of his innings had gone unnoticed – even by us on the field. But Miandad's mind was ticking all the while, waiting to seize the opportunity.

A year later, Pakistan were in India, and I had a run-in with him after we had won the Hyderabad ODI. It was a close match and had Abdul Qadir not attempted a second run on the last ball of the innings with the scores equal, the match would have been a tie. As it happened, Pakistan lost 7 wickets to our 6, and according to the playing conditions, the match was awarded to us. This didn't go down well with Miandad. After the match, he came to our dressing room, insisting loudly that we had won because of cheating. With adrenaline still pumping, I couldn't take Miandad's jibes, picked up a shoe and chased him back into his dressing room, where Imran Khan intervened and brought peace.

The altercation was quickly forgotten, however. When the teams were travelling for the next match, we spent time together on the flight. The incident never featured in any conversation then or later.

Though he had to live in the shadow of Imran Khan, Miandad was a very shrewd captain. His cricketing brain was second to none, and, as Imran's lieutenant, contributed a lot to his success. As personalities, the two were a study in contrast: Imran, aloof and imperious; Miandad, always in the thick of it, a confrontationist, so to speak. Together, they made a formidable duo.

Miandad knew every rule in the book and how far he could push the envelope. He made it a point to know everything about his opponents. He would find out about them through the grapevine and detect vulnerabilities in players within minutes of their being on the field.

Off the field, Miandad was a different personality from what most people imagine. He was friendly and jovial, a prankster who could bring the house down with his jokes, anecdotes and mimicry. But on the field, all friendship vanished. He was combative to the core, the kind of player you would rather have on your own side than against.

HIS LORDSHIP

Dilip Vengsarkar

Dilip Vengsarkar is rightly called the 'lord of Lord's'. He made three successive Test centuries at the hallowed ground in 1979, 1982 and 1986. He looked good for yet another in 1990 too. We batted together for several overs in this match and I could see how determined he was to reach this milestone. He looked in complete control until he fell, unfortunately, after a polished 52.

Nonetheless, three centuries on the same ground is an extraordinary achievement. There is no rational explanation why some batsmen score heavily on certain grounds. But it does happen. And if these centuries come at the most famous venue in the sport, it turns the world's attention on you.

Two of Dilip's centuries at Lord's, in 1982 and 1986, I watched as a member of the Indian team. The second one was particularly special as the pitch was loaded in favour of bowlers. But he stood up to the challenge with steady nerves and sound technique. His innings was instrumental in India winning the Test, which at one stage looked like it could have gone the other way.

Dilip's best overseas effort, however, came on a different ground during the same tour. In the second Test at Headingley in 1986, conditions were even better for pace bowlers and the hardship for batsmen consequently greater. The pitch was seam friendly throughout and, for Indian players at least, the weather was wretchedly cold.

Apart from Dilip, no other batsman from either side topped 50. He made 61 and 102 in the two innings. It was a fantastic display of batsmanship, a masterclass in the handling of swing and seam movement. On that tour, he didn't put a foot wrong. In fact, he was the main reason why India could win a series in England after thirty-one years.

Between 1985 and 1987, Dilip was in his pomp. Though rankings and ratings were yet to be introduced, he was easily among the top three batsmen in the world at the time. Mind you, this was no mean achievement considering Sunil Gavaskar, Javed Miandad, Viv Richards, Gordon Greenidge, Mohinder Amarnath, Graham Gooch, David Gower and Martin Crowe were still around.

Dilip and I played a lot of cricket together for Tatas, Bombay, West Zone and India, and shared many partnerships in which I got to observe him very closely. He was a 'confidence' player. Not the best starter, but once in the groove, he could produce bountiful runs with his wide range of strokes. His batting was built around a tight and compact technique. He was a very good reader of pitches and would adjust to the conditions, no matter how challenging, quickly. In England, he cut down on his backlift and follow-through, held the bat very close to his body and played the ball late. In sunnier climes, he would get more expansive in strokes and style. He revelled on bad tracks. On a very poor Cuttack pitch in 1986, he made 166 against Sri Lanka when all other batsmen struggled or threw their bats around riskily.

Dilip was unafraid of pace and short-pitched bowling, willing to counter-attack, and always looking to dominate the bowling. He used his height and reach quite superbly in playing spin, either from the crease or dancing down the pitch. His front foot drives on either side of the wicket could be majestic and had a special appeal for fans. I firmly believe he didn't do full justice to his talent. He should have got 1,800–2,000 runs more, and certainly not have been restricted to just four centuries overseas, all of them in England.

Dilip's insights in the dressing room were always valued, as indeed his ability to give opposing batsmen 'lip' when fielding close in. He and Miandad would inevitably have a go at each other from silly point when the other was batting. Miandad was a tease and mimic, but Dilip has a wicked sense of humour and can come up with pungent one-liners without prompting. He would give back as good as he got. But off the field, they were buddies.

One player who saw red every time he saw Dilip was Malcolm Marshall. For some reason, Dilip always got under Macko's skin. The contest between them would be high-octane and exciting to watch. But not so for the rest of us in the Indian dressing room, for he always seemed to get the best out of Macko which put us under pressure too!

Dilip's captaincy stint was all too brief. Two of the three series he led in were against Viv Richards's West Indies, then the best side in the world. In the home series in 1987, he was unwell for the third Test at Madras, and I was given the opportunity to captain the India team. After the away series in the Caribbean, he fell afoul of the authorities and lost the captaincy.

His contribution to Indian cricket didn't end with his retirement, though. In his 'second innings', Dilip has put in splendid effort in coaching and nurturing youngsters through his academy, been an administrator in Mumbai Cricket Association, and also an excellent national selector, making some very interesting and important choices that have served Indian cricket well.

Dilip was my first room partner when I made my debut in New Zealand in 1980-81; we retired in the same year; and have lived in the same apartment complex for more than two decades. It's been my privilege to have been in this long partnership with him.

ALL-ROUNDER PAR EXCELLENCE

Ian Botham

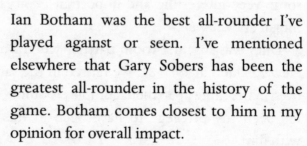

Ian Botham was the best all-rounder I've played against or seen. I've mentioned elsewhere that Gary Sobers has been the greatest all-rounder in the history of the game. Botham comes closest to him in my opinion for overall impact.

My earliest memory of Botham is from watching a match at the Wankhede Stadium. This was the Jubilee Test in January 1980, celebrating fifty years of cricket between India and England. I particularly wanted to see him bowl because even in my late teens I had fancied myself as a fast bowler of sorts, though my stock-in-trade was spin.

Botham took centre stage in the Test almost from start to finish. Bowling at full tilt, he picked up 6 wickets. India finished with a moderate score of 242, but when England were reduced to 58 for 5, it did not seem such a bad score after all. With his side tottering, Botham took charge with a swashbuckling century that brought England back into the match. He found an ally in Bob Taylor, whom captain Gundappa Viswanath reprieved by overruling the umpire's decision for a caught behind. As I would discover when I joined the team, that was just like Vishy. Would I have done the same thing in his place? Certainly not!

In India's second innings, Botham bowled with hostility and stamina, using the cross breeze from the Arabian Sea to get a pronounced late swing. With 7 wickets in this innings, he had 13 in the match, and a blazing century in between. I had never seen such a spectacular all-round performance. Botham was India's destroyer and my new hero.

He would do one better in the 1981 Ashes. I was in England with the Under-19 team when Botham became the toast of his country by turning the tables on arch-rivals Australia in stunning fashion after his team was forced to follow on at Headingley and defeat looked certain. Botham scored 50, 149 not out, and took 7 wickets in the match.

Captaincy taken away from him, career almost at rock bottom, then Mike Brearley speaks some golden words in his ear, which changes the destiny of the series as well as Botham's. It is difficult to imagine how one player could influence the course of a six-Test series so dramatically.

He always loved the big stage and, in the wake of these exploits, Botham became a larger-than-life persona, drawing awe and admiration everywhere he played. Next to Australia, playing against India seemed to bring out the best in him.

In 1981-82, I was in the team that played England. It wasn't a particularly gratifying series for spectators with both teams locked in a defensive mindset. Botham's aggressive knocks did liven things up every now and then, though what impressed me more was his incredible bowling: long spells in hot conditions on unhelpful pitches. He had a great natural outswinger which could fell even the most in-form batsmen. Built like an ox, he remained seemingly tireless despite long spells of bowling. Stories swirled around about his nocturnal adventures, but there wasn't a single day on the field when he wasn't trying to dominate with bat or ball.

In 1982, when we toured England, he pulverized us with a century and a double century in the second and third Tests, and picked up crucial wickets in the three-Test series. I was bowling when Botham drove the ball straight into Sunil Gavaskar's leg at short leg, instantly terminating his series. It didn't look like a particularly powerful stroke, but this belies Botham's strength. Even his defensive prods carried great power. And if you wanted more evidence of this, a handshake would be enough.

What Botham did with bat and ball, the catches he took, the matches he won, sets him apart from anyone else in the era he played in, or even subsequently. He had serious competition, of course, from Richard Hadlee, Imran Khan and Kapil Dev, all of whom may have been better than him in one or the other aspects of the game at different points in time. But when you view the whole package, and his ability to win matches for England, especially when the chips were down, the scales tilt towards Botham. Sheer statistics tell you why he was special. He got more runs than his rival all-rounders, scored more centuries than any of them, took 382 wickets and over 100 catches with his bucket-like hands.

When I joined Glamorgan as a professional in 1987, the best names in cricket were part of the county circuit, and the three biggest were Botham, Viv Richards and Imran Khan. Even out of these three, I think Botham put most bums on the seats in his heyday.

Post our playing days, we've spent some fun times in England, or in India when he's come down for television work. He was a flamboyant player and is a large-hearted man, living life king-size both on and off the field.

KAPIL DA JAWAB NAHIN!

Kapil Dev

 Kapil Dev was the most talented of the four great all-rounders of my era. Fans of Ian Botham, Imran Khan and Richard Hadlee might not agree, but having watched and played against all – including Kapil in domestic cricket over several years – I stand firm by my assessment.

Kapil was a marvellous swing bowler, brilliant attacking batsman and superb fielder. Imran was a more organized batsman, Hadlee a technically more accomplished bowler, and Botham was certainly more flamboyant in all aspects of the game. But when you look at Kapil Dev's career in its entirety – his accomplishments and his contribution to India's successes as a player – you get a better perspective of his talent and the impact he had on Indian cricket.

For a fast bowler from India to take 400-plus Test wickets seems surreal even now. Add to this his 5,000-plus runs and it becomes unreal. These stats highlight not just Kapil's contribution to Indian cricket, but also establish him as an all-time great in the annals of the game.

He was a supreme athlete, naturally fit and robust, capable of bowling long spells without complaint. I hardly ever saw him leave the field because he was fatigued. I can remember only two occasions when he missed a contest. One was in 1984, when he had to skip the Asia Cup because of a knee surgery, and the other was in the 1984-85 home season, when he was controversially dropped for the Calcutta Test against David Gower's team; a decision which still evokes debate. Had he not been dropped for this Test, Kapil would have played 132 Tests on the trot. To be able to sustain form and fitness for so long was perhaps the most remarkable part of his career. I can't think of too many cricketers who played sixteen years without a break. Certainly not all-rounders, and more so a team's leading fast bowler.

In an era dominated by the likes of Clive Lloyd, Ian Botham, Viv Richards, Gordon Greenidge and Graham Gooch, Kapil made a name for himself as one of the hardest and cleanest strikers of the ball. I remember a match against the West Indies in Nagpur where he sent a Patrick Patterson delivery rocketing to the fence and it ricocheted back to the bowler. Patterson wasn't amused.

An instinctive and aggressive batsman, Kapil was always on the lookout for quick runs. But he wasn't a senseless slogger. He relished big shots and most of his strokes came from hits through the line, usually smack from the middle of the bat. He was also a superb runner between wickets, which put additional pressure on the fielding side. He didn't plan his innings. There was no deep analysis. (That came when he started doing commentary!) He was a terrific improviser, and had an excellent eye and reflexes. For someone who played so aggressively, he was astonishingly good in tough situations, difficult conditions and pitches.

In the only Test I captained, against the West Indies in Madras in 1988, Kapil got a superb match-winning century on a track that had something in it for bowlers right through. A year earlier on the same ground, he had hit a stroke-filled century against Australia in the Tied Test which kept us alive in the match. There were other memorable knocks too. Against England at Lord's in 1990, he made a breathtaking 77, tonking Eddie Hemmings down the ground for four consecutive sixes to avoid the follow on. In 1992, at Port Elizabeth, South Africa, he hit a rousing century in a losing cause, sending Allan Donald and Co. scrambling all over the park. Not just centuries, there were several half-centuries too from his bat, which made big impact in Tests.

The innings which immortalized Kapil is obviously his 175 not out against Zimbabwe in the 1983 World Cup. It is among the most extraordinary ODI innings for the daunting circumstances in which it was played. We were caught on a vicious seaming track at Tunbridge Wells. The top order fell in a heap, leaving us precariously placed. I remember being sixth out, when the score was just 20-odd. Kapil took maybe ten or fifteen minutes to settle down, and then suddenly his batting changed. Once he had got his eye in, nothing fazed him. Whether fast, medium pace or slow, the Zimbabwe bowlers came under heavy attack as he kept depositing the ball into the car park.

His stupendous innings turned the match on its head, and triggered fresh ambition in the side, culminating in us beating the West Indies in the final to win the title. Kapil's role in this triumph was salutary. He led from the front at every opportunity. If his innings against Zimbabwe revived our fortunes and our appetite for victory midway through the tournament, the catch in the final, a steepling skier, to dismiss a rampaging Viv Richards virtually sealed the final. His sunny personality, always brimming with optimism, was infectious and rubbed off on us all through the tournament.

I've spent many words extolling Kapil's batting, but it was his bowling which had a larger influence on Indian cricket. No Indian pace bowler before him had taken 100 Test wickets. In fact, pace bowlers were few and far in between, and those who played for India barely survived a few years. Kapil's arrival was transformational. Overt dependence on spin ended with him. India's use of the new ball was no longer just perfunctory, but became a weapon.

An outstanding outswing bowler, accuracy and control were his greatest strengths, and very rarely did I see him being taken apart by any batsman anywhere. Unlike his batting, which was spontaneous, in bowling, Kapil applied measure and method to prey on batsmen, invariably making early inroads into the opposition's batting. He was technically perfect and classical in approach, leap and delivery stride, bowling from very close to the stumps, getting the ball to swing late both ways.

The outswinger was particularly deadly and got him many famous victims. Few fast bowlers have used the grip and the seam better than him. Just how good he was is evident in his success on heartbreak home pitches where fast bowlers have generally struggled, and against the terrific batting line-ups of Pakistan, West Indies, Australia and England – both at home and away. Had he got some more support from the other end, and with better close-in catching, Kapil's stats may have been more impressive.

His biggest contribution to Indian cricket was in sparking off a fast bowling revolution in the country. If India has a dozen pace bowlers to choose from today, it is because of Kapil Dev's influence in the 1980s on young cricketers coming up the ranks.

I played my entire Test career with Kapil Dev in the team and shared a warm relationship with him. We had our run-ins, but that was only because of Bombay v Haryana or West Zone v North in domestic cricket, which was always a grudge contest. Otherwise, his brilliance as an all-rounder always had me in awe.

An amusing thing about Kapil was his reluctance to speak in Hindi, which came naturally to him. At all times, and specially in press conferences, he would insist on talking in English. What he said could be misconstrued by those around him, but Kapil didn't care. I too would answer all questions in English, even those asked in Hindi, but today, when it comes to describing Kapil, I can only borrow the ad line which he made famous with his exploits: 'Kapil Dev da jawaab nahin!'

TERMINATOR

Malcolm Marshall

I rate my centuries in the West Indies in 1983 and 1989 as the most gratifying of my career. In that period, the West Indies had a hostile all-pace attack that was difficult to play anywhere, but even more so on their home pitches.

The pick of the West Indies bowlers in my time was Malcolm Marshall. He joined the team a few years after Andy Roberts, Michael Holding and Joel Garner, integrated himself with these classy bowlers to form a fearsome foursome, and swiftly surpassed them in wickets and skills.

If you travel the world and ask the leading batsmen of that era about the bowlers they were most intimidated by, I am sure several of them will point in the same direction. Many of them might still be bearing scars from facing him on the field.

If they got a fair few runs against him, like I did, these became landmarks to cherish forever.

Not as tall as the typical West Indies fast bowler, Macko was no less menacing. He bowled at a torrid pace and with a fire that just wouldn't die down, whether in his first spell of the day or last. On any surface, he would get his deliveries to skid through because of his bowling action. He literally sprinted in to bowl, itself a frightening sight, and combined with his whippy action, it gave batsmen very little time to adjust to line and length.

Like Wasim Akram, he was not dependent on help from the pitch. He could swing the ball at extreme pace, vary his length, and change the line by going over or round the wicket without losing control. Round the wicket, he was particularly nasty because the line was very difficult to pick. His accuracy meant there was little respite for batsmen. We survived his overs on tenterhooks.

When there was no assistance for swing or seam, he would bowl just short of length, using his shoulders and back to get extra bounce, getting the ball to snort at the batsman. Physics tells us all deliveries will lose velocity after pitching. In Macko's case, this was marginal. Unlike for most bowlers, Macko's bouncer would hasten off the pitch. That was the impression one got even if it seemed scientifically impossible. Most times, this would be a 'throat ball', but occasionally, as the unfortunate Mike Gatting realized when he had to pick up the debris of his shattered nose from the pitch after he had failed to fend off a short-pitched delivery, it would go for the face. In the 1983 World Cup, Macko's ball hit Dilip Vengsarkar on the mouth, terminating Dilip's appearances in the tournament.

In both my centuries in the West Indies – at Antigua in 1983, playing in the middle order, and Bridgetown in 1989 at number three after Navjot Sidhu had been dismissed first ball – Macko put me to severe test, with pace, late movement and a generous sprinkling of bouncers. He kept me guessing with his length too, drawing me on to the front foot, pushing me back, constantly probing with subtle changes.

We got Macko at his best in two series in 1983, home and away, and he was the vital difference between the two sides, particularly on slow Indian pitches. It is my opinion that from the quartet of great West Indies fast bowlers, Marshall troubled Sunil Gavaskar the most. I can offer Macko no greater tribute, as Sunny was the master technician at that time. That I lasted on the field against him raised my own self-esteem by several notches and, I guess, gathered his respect too, for we would often discuss batsmanship and batsmen.

Like Imran Khan bowling at his peak in the 1980s, Macko cleaned up every team that he played against in that era. He did so for a longer time, without sledging or abusing batsmen, but he did have a menacing glare for those who hit him for a boundary or so. He just hated conceding runs.

His presence on the field would electrify fans, especially in the Caribbean, and specifically in his hometown, Barbados, where he was a cult hero. I can still hear the raucous Saturday crowd cheering Macko past Lance Gibbs's record as the highest wicket-taker for West Indies. He was 3 wickets short when the Test began and when he claimed his fourth, Kensington Oval exploded.

Our rivalry on the field was intense, but off it, we became very good friends. Without ball in hand, Macko was a genial bloke with a lively sense of humour. He once came to my house in Sportsfield Building with Des Haynes. My Bombay colleague Alan Sippy played barman to indulgence, and together the two Bajans brought the roof down, prompting Sunny Gavaskar to come down three stories from his apartment to check on why the loud laughter sounded so familiar. He ended up joining Macko, Dessie, Alan and me for a long night of fun and banter.

Alas, Macko left this planet too early.

NEVER SAY DIE

Allan Border

Allan Border is a man of few words and magnificent deeds: a hero, without the accompanying brouhaha, for his batting, but also how he led Australian cricket from despondency to eminence as captain.

I learnt a lot from Border – and Javed Miandad – about how to approach the sport, and borrowed a lot from them to improve my own game. These guys had a core of steel and played hard, in fact even with meanness, in the middle. An early lesson was that you can't be namby-pamby when playing at the highest level. Batting, for instance, is not just about technique, style and flair; it is also about making runs when they matter most, even if not attractive to everybody. You don't play sport to win over admirers but to win matches.

Another – and equally important – thing I learnt from Border was to leave the pressures and bitterness of battle behind on the field after stumps have been drawn for the day. We've had our share of sledges and verbal jousts, but once the match was over, he would be the first to offer a beer. And advice for any young cricketer, which I latched on to eagerly in my early years. We've shared as much time in rival dressing rooms, as with each other after a day's play or between matches.

Border came into the side at a time when Australian cricket was doddering. The best names had defected to the World Series Cricket, and selectors were looking here, there, everywhere for replacements. Border was among the dozen or so young players blooded in international cricket in this period. However, only a few of them went on to leave a lasting impact on the sport, and only one – Steve Waugh, who came in the mid-1980s – played for as long and as prolifically as Border.

The batting stats of Border and Waugh are fairly similar, and both men captained Australia. If Waugh shows up as a more successful captain it is because bald figures don't provide context to situational hardships that demand leadership skills in a match, a series or an era.

Border's captaincy period is a major inflection point in Australian cricket. When he took over, the team was in the doldrums. By the time he retired, he had led Australia to a World Cup win (1987) and also helped recover substantial ground that had been lost in Test cricket.

As a new captain put in the hot seat for which he was hardly prepared, it wasn't easy for Border. His story is as much about trying to actualize his own talent and ambition as coping with apprehensions about a team he had taken charge of in extenuating circumstances, after his predecessor, Kim Hughes, quit in tears.

Border wasn't a unanimous choice as captain. The media was hostile to him because he wasn't a natural communicator. He was thought to be diffident, or worse, lacking imagination as a captain. But that was far from the truth. I saw Border's nerve and grit first-hand at the memorable Tied Test against Australia at Madras in 1986, the toughest match I've ever played.

The see-saw battle put all twenty-two players in the match to severe scrutiny, but it was the captains who were under most pressure. Though I still maintain that umpire Dara Dotiwalla made a mistake in giving Maninder Singh leg before wicket, bringing the Indian innings to an end one run short of victory, there is also no doubt that had Border not maintained his composure and trusted his bowlers right till the end, the Aussies might have lost the match much earlier.

The 1987 World Cup victory that followed soon after catapulted Border to greater heights as a batsman and brought him enormous respect as captain. His handling of a young side that beat Pakistan in the semi-finals and England in the final – among the biggest upsets in cricket history – was exemplary.

One doesn't associate 'style' with Border's batting; dogged, gritty, brave, stodgy, sticky are adjectives that come to mind readily. Let me add two more: lion-hearted and versatile. He was at his best when circumstances were most daunting.

The runs he scored against – and in – the West Indies, then the premier side in the world, his twin 150-plus knocks in Pakistan, and several impressive innings in India are testimony to this. As is his time in England, of course, where he batted with huge success for Australia, Essex and Gloucestershire.

In the latter half of his career, Border became a father figure
to a whole generation of Aussie cricketers who would have been
the poorer without his mentoring. He was largely instrumental
in shaping the career of Shane Warne, Australia's highest wicket-
taker in Tests.

There have undoubtedly been bigger stars in Australian
cricket, with better batting averages and win percentages as
captain. But when you consider his overall contribution to the
sport, Border stands on a pedestal all of his own.

*He was an artist. He didn't build an innings,
he painted one. The longer it lasted, the more
beautiful and breathtaking it became.*

GUNDAPPA
VISWANATH

FAROKH
ENGINEER

*To my ten year-old self, Farokh seemed a fantastic action
hero, scoring at a scorching pace, taking diving catches
and effecting lightning-quick stumpings.*

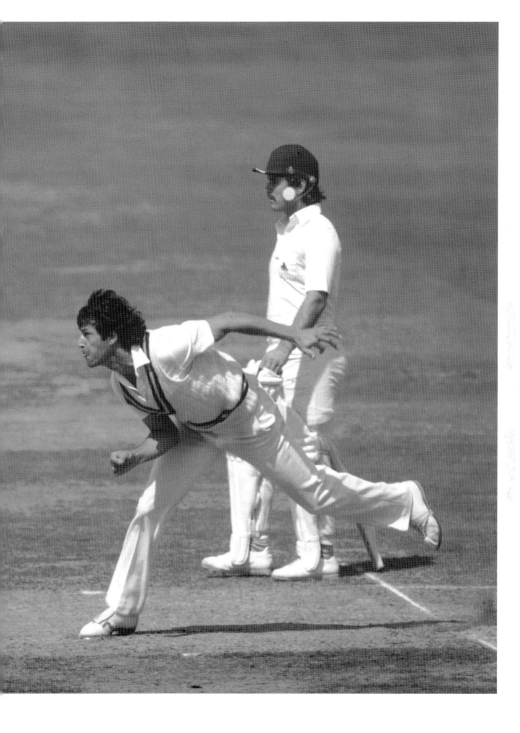

He also seemed to be at his most aggressive against
India. I realized what a fierce competitor he could be
through a couple of exchanges in the middle.

IMRAN

KHAN

ALLAN
BORDER

His handling of a young side that beat England in the
[1987 World Cup] final – among the biggest upsets in
cricket history – was exemplary.

I had several years playing hard cricket against him and he was always looking to hit my stumps, head or toes! He never gave an inch.

WASIM
AKRAM

ANIL
KUMBLE

Anil became the second bowler in cricket history to take all 10 wickets in an innings. What came through was not just his exemplary control, but also aggressive intent.

He was a majestic batsman. When in full
form, he batted like a prince, with regal
strokes from a dazzlingly rich repertoire.

MARTIN
CROWE

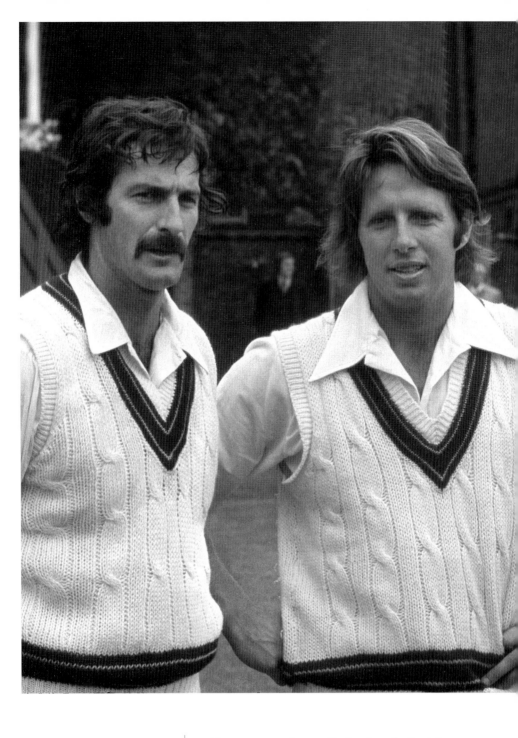

DENNIS LILLEE

JEFF THOMSON

There were several young fast bowlers who fancied themselves a Lillee or a Thomson. I, too, was one of them, though I bowled left-handed.

*He looked to be in an even more murderous
mood against us in the 1983 World Cup final,
smashing the bowling to all parts of Lord's.*

VIVIAN
RICHARDS

KAPIL DEV

If India has a dozen pace bowlers to choose from today, it is because of Kapil Dev's influence in the 1980s on young cricketers coming up the ranks.

Dilip has a wicked sense of humour and can come up with pungent one-liners without prompting. He would give back as good as he got.

DILIP
VENGSARKAR

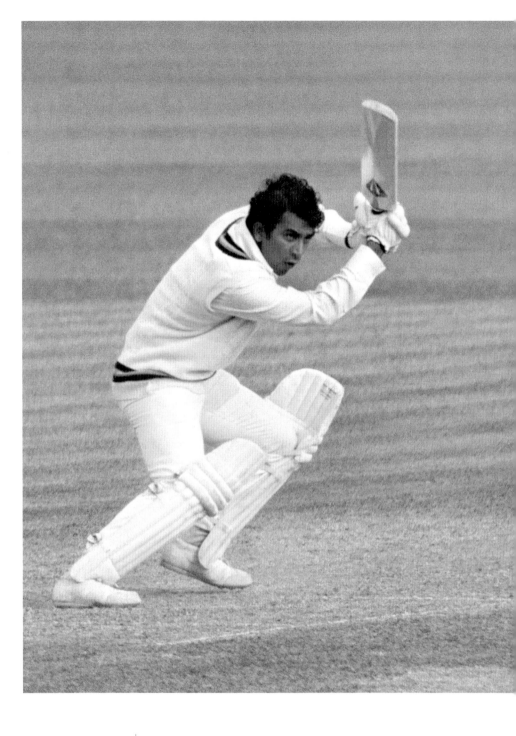

SUNIL
GAVASKAR

He put his head down for his first 20-odd runs and then became machine-like as he jogged past milestones of 50, 100, 150 and 200 without blemish or sweat.

*It is unfortunate that Greg's tenure became
controversial and was brief, for he had all
the credentials to make a big impact.*

GREG
CHAPPELL

MALCOLM
MARSHALL

He literally sprinted in to bowl, itself a frightening
sight, and with his whippy action gave batsmen
very little time to adjust to line and length.

He made his Test debut in Pakistan in 1989
when only sixteen ... battling against
Imran Khan, Wasim Akram and Waqar Younis.

SACHIN
TENDULKAR

KUMAR
SANGAKKARA

He commanded all the strokes in the book, but what
I fancied most was the cover drive, played inside out.
It could destroy the confidence of any bowler.

We were not only wary of Jonty, but scared of him.
Even if he was positioned a little deeper, we would
avoid taking a run if the ball was hit in his direction.

JONTY

RHODES

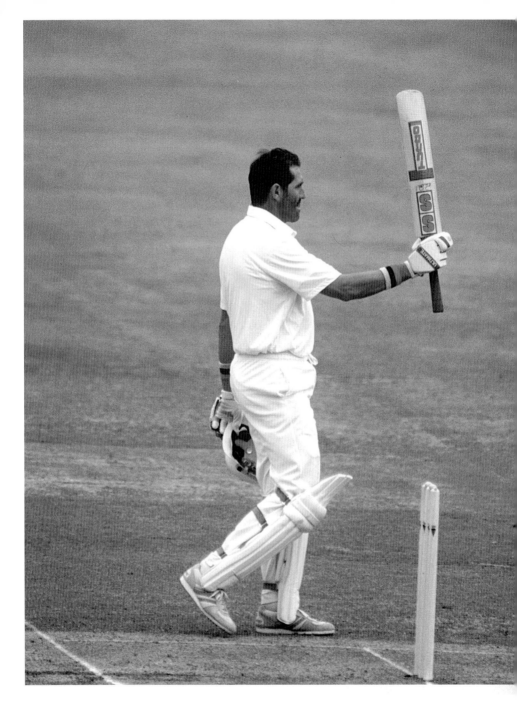

GRAHAM
GOOCH

*He played every stroke you can think of as we threw
our all at him and went on to score 333, showing our
bowlers and fielders every inch of the Lord's ground.*

At a time when it looked like slow bowlers were becoming history, he, Muttiah Muralitharan and Anil Kumble helped revive spin bowling.

SHANE
WARNE

RAHUL
DRAVID

The bounce and pace of the Aussie attack didn't unsettle him, nor did the sledging. Opponents recognized the futility of trying to needle him.

His unflappable temperament was something that bemused me at first, then amazed me as I realized it wasn't a put on.

MAHENDRA
SINGH DHONI

R. ASHWIN

RAVINDRA JADEJA

India's dominance at home in the last seven or eight years, apart from runs and centuries scored by top-order batsmen, is primarily because of Ashwin and Jadeja.

He is fired up all time, which some see as effrontery to cricket's etiquette, but he never lets his natural aggression conflict with his professional instinct.

VIRAT
KOHLI

Champion of Champions, Benson and
Hedges World Series, 1985.

ELEGANCE AT PLAY

David Gower

Left-handers are generally very attractive to watch, but even among them, David Gower was the most elegant I've seen. He never hit the ball, he stroked it, with timing, finesse and grace that left one spellbound.

Tall and upright, he had a lovely relaxed stance from which he would launch into defence or attack with such ease that it almost seemed casual. He was often taken to task by the English media for being too laid-back – as both batsman and captain – when in fact, he was anything but.

We played a lot of cricket against each other between 1981 and 1990 – in Tests and county cricket – and he never came across as someone who wasn't serious about what he did on the field, be it batting, fielding or captaining the team.

Gower could be a fierce competitor as I saw for myself when England toured India in 1984-85. I captained the Under-25 team against Gower's side at Ahmedabad, and watched him wrestle with his own batting, as well as the struggles of other batsmen. He looked in scratchy form in the first innings, the timing awry and footwork sluggish. There was no pace in the pitch and he hit one straight back to me as the ball stopped a bit.

Captains always look for vulnerability in opponents, and it seemed to me that Gower, England's best batsman, was not in the best form. We won that match by an innings, sixteen-year-old leg spinner Laxman Sivaramakrishnan exposing England's frailty against spin.

Word spread quickly, and I added my own bit to Sunil Gavaskar, who was captaining the Indian team, which included young Siva too. In the first Test in Bombay, our target was Gower; we wanted him for as few runs as possible. Kapil Dev dismissed him in the first innings and, in the second, I had him caught close in. Siva took 12 wickets on debut, England collapsed and we won by eight wickets.

After that first Test, Gower was a beleaguered batsman and captain. There was nothing to suggest that a recovery from this situation was possible, so comprehensive had been our win. Yet, despite the loss and his own inadequate performance, Gower recovered from there to lead England to one of its finest overseas campaigns, and beat us 2–1. There have been subsequent instances when a series has been turned on its head in India (2001: India beat Australia 2–1 after losing the first Test; 2013: England beat India 2–1 after losing the first Test; 2020: India beat Australia 2–1 after losing the first Test), but the 1984-85 England team was the first to breach this hurdle.

Gower made this possible through patience and astute planning, neither of which he is given enough credit for. The team under him wasn't the strongest. But he got the best out of his players, especially spinners Pat Pocock and Phil Edmonds, to turn the tables on us. Perhaps playing away from home helped Gower. In England, his poor batting form might have compelled a change in captaincy. In India, he had the latitude to bring his tactical and man-management skills to the fore even as runs deserted him.

In that series, Gower scored just 167 runs, and overall, in India, he scored 558 runs in twelve Tests, which is just about modest. But it would be misleading to believe he wasn't adept at playing on slow turners. Factor in 449 runs in three Tests against Pakistan and 131 in a solitary Test against Sri Lanka, and it is evident how good he actually was against spin on slow, turning tracks.

This was because he was such a good judge of length. When one talks of Gower's batting, it is his aristocratic cover drives that dominate the conversation, but when bowling to him, I found he was brilliant at the cut and pull strokes as well, because he could read the length so well and so early – probably why he was so successful in Australia and the West Indies.

Gower was always under the scanner as captain. He was thought to be a tad frivolous, and without the capacity to harness the team because some critics reckoned he was self-indulgent. This was utterly ridiculous. He was individualistic, but only with the bat; it did not come from a place of self-centredness. He was a stylist with a capacity for risk-taking that doesn't come easily to batsmen who think averages all the time. As a captain, he was not overly aggressive, but sound in dealing with prickly situations and teammates.

I'd agree, as far as cricketers are concerned, that he was a non-conformist. Not in terms of batting technique, but in his outlook to the game and life in general. He loved and lived the good life. Cricket for him was a task but also fun. His natty dress sense, passion for wine and fine dining added to the aura of his personality, but he didn't let fame or money go to his head.

We quit around the same time, but commentary frequently brought us together. He is a fine reader of the game, and even when he was critical of a player or a team's performance, he expressed it with balance and empathy. A droll, sophisticated sense of humour endeared him as much to fellow commentators as to fans.

Gower is a thorough gentleman and a great ambassador for England wherever he goes.

PRINCE AMONG BATSMEN

Martin Crowe

Martin Crowe was one of my closest friends among overseas players. We were of the same vintage, played against each other several times in the 1980s, and our friendship lasted almost forty years till he was cruelly snatched away by cancer.

The fundamental job of batsmen is to score runs any which way, but if these come with poise, grace and elan, these are cherished even more. Martin belonged to this category: technically sound, not a dour run accumulator, but with strokes of beauty and finesse. He was a majestic batsman. When in full form, he batted like a prince, with regal strokes from a dazzlingly rich repertoire. He was particularly impressive off the front foot, on either side of the wicket, leaning into his drives with ease, the timing and balance supreme.

I've seen Martin hit what seemed like unplayable yorkers through the covers, leaving the bowler seething at such temerity, or throwing up his hands in helpless resignation. Given a little width or a slightly shorter delivery, he would cut, hook or pull with ferocity. The margin for error when bowling against him was miniscule.

Masters of pace and swing like Wasim Akram and Waqar Younis rate him very highly too. They tell me he read swing and reverse swing superbly, which allowed him to get into proper position, whereas other batsmen would be wrong-footed. Because of his short backlift, strong forearms and ability to judge length early, Martin was able to score runs off deliveries that most batsmen would struggle to even defend.

Like all great batsmen, he liked to dominate bowlers, but also knew when this was most opportune. He was equally good against pace and spin. The better the bowlers, the greater his ambition to score runs, and the more sparkling his stroke play. It is significant that his best performances came against Australia, Pakistan and the West Indies – teams that had the best bowling attacks in the 1980s.

He was ahead of his time in devising methods to make New Zealand succeed when he was captain. In the 1991-92 World Cup, from which I crashed out very early because my knees gave away, he made Mark Greatbatch into a pinch-hitter and opened the bowling with off-spinner Dipak Patel. I followed the tournament closely and was unsure whether these unorthodox tactics would work. They did, and marvellously so! With Martin himself in magnificent form, New Zealand looked the best team in the tournament till they were upstaged by Pakistan in the semi-final. Pinch-hitting openers and slow bowlers using the new ball, however, have become accepted strategy in limited-overs cricket now.

When he came to India in 1995, around the end of his career, he went through a lean trot. I had retired by then, and we caught up often on that tour, generally talking about where the game was headed. This seemed to be uppermost in his mind. I had always found Martin to be a radical thinker. He had preceded me in county cricket by many years, and his analyses of different players on the circuit, or how to survive the gruelling demands of non-stop cricket, were always thought-provoking, if offbeat.

Even when he retired, Martin's passion for cricket didn't dim. He was a thinker and theoretician, trying to find ways and means to make cricket even more popular. He was way ahead of anybody else in this, proposing innovations like six-a-side and eight-a-side tournaments. Not everything he suggested found favour with authority, or was completely doable, but this didn't stop him from coming up with new ideas.

Temperamentally, he could be fiery and inflexible, unlike his brother, Jeff, who has also been a friend, and with whom I've spent many evenings when he's been on duty as match referee and I've been part of the commentary team. On several issues about the game, he would be unflinchingly stubborn. It was 'my way or the highway' with Martin if you disagreed. I didn't have many reasons to, though, for I found his ideas interesting and progressive.

With cricket undergoing so many innovations these days, his mind would have been invaluable. Sadly, Martin Crowe went too soon.

MAN OF DESTINY

Arjuna Ranatunga

I was in the Under-19 India team that toured Sri Lanka in 1979. The island country hadn't yet got Test status, but informal cricket exchanges between our countries were fairly frequent.

By this time, the BCCI – as I was to gather later – was pushing for full membership for Sri Lanka in the ICC. While that would take a year or so more to come into fruition, junior-level cricket between our two countries became regular and took place in a more structured manner.

In one of the matches at Colombo during the 1979 tour, after the fall of the second wicket, the batsman who came in at number four was a chubby youngster. He had a nice pot belly, and walked to the wicket with a waddle, twirling his bat.

While he was taking guard from the umpire, there were some jokes exchanged among our players (mainly in Hindi, so as not to be rude), mocking the batsman's expansive girth, and how he did not look like a sportsperson at all and so should be easy to dismiss.

The smiles and jokes vanished swiftly when the left-hander started to bat. A couple of overs to get his eye in, and after that he simply decimated our bowling, smashing a brilliant hundred that left the bowlers with wounded egos and fielders sore from chasing leather. Those of us who played that match knew then itself that Arjuna Ranatunga was a special talent, someone who would play for his country sooner rather than later.

Over the next fifteen years, India and Sri Lanka met each other often. In all those contests, Arjuna Ranatunga was the biggest thorn in our side. I got to know him extremely well during this time, which helped me understand why he was so successful as a batsman; more importantly, what made him the fine captain he was and the big influence he left on the game.

As a batsman, Arjuna was hardly a stylist. His defensive strokes were ungainly jabs, and drives in front of the wicket lacked the finesse and grace normally associated with left-handers. But this did not mean he was error-prone. In fact, he was among the most resourceful batsmen I've seen or bowled to.

Because he was a fine reader of pitches and conditions, he could adjust and adapt swiftly. If you thought he was slow on his feet because of his girth, he could surprise you with his speed while running between wickets or while fielding.

He favoured horizontal bat strokes. The cut, pull and hook came readily to him because he was very good on the back foot. He was also exceptional at playing the sweep against spinners – always crucial on tricky subcontinental tracks. He had a strong streak to improvise too. Once set, he was difficult to contain.

I'll sharpen – and shorten – this description to say Arjuna was a left-handed Javed Miandad, in his batting as well as mindset for the game. Like Miandad, he was cheeky and street-smart in everything he did on the field. He was driven by pragmatic pursuit of survival and run-scoring, uncaring about niceties of classical technique. He never ever had his tail between his legs, was always ready for a scrap even against the strongest opponents, and relished playing on the nerves of his rivals.

Where Arjuna differed vastly from Miandad was in captaincy. Few understood and read the game better than Miandad. Arjuna went a step ahead in this as a leader who commanded the respect of his team and had a vision on how to take Sri Lankan cricket ahead.

Arjuna was a tough character who made his country – players and fans – believe they could take on the world. Till he became captain, the Sri Lankans were thought to be splendidly talented cricketers, but softies, and not very good at handling pressure.

Arjuna changed that by personal example in the fearless way he batted, but even more so with the way he motivated his team members and stood by them in crises. That is the hallmark of a leader, and such guys always have my admiration.

His support for Muttiah Muralitharan, who was called out for chucking in Australia in 1995, was stormy and unsavoury, but changed the way the world perceived Sri Lankan cricket. The clear signal Arjuna sent out was he wasn't going to be bullied.

His captaincy in the 1996 World Cup was masterly. He was the one to spot Sanath Jayasuriya's potential as a destructive opener, and made Romesh Kaluwitharana his partner in the tournament. One-day cricket had seen a pinch-hitting opener, but two together was new, and wreaked havoc on opponents.

The self-belief he instilled in the dressing room saw Sri Lanka pull off their staggering win.

His entry into politics after he retired didn't surprise me. In cricket, Arjuna clearly enjoyed handling the power and responsibility that came with captaincy. It fed his intellect, kept him involved in the play and allowed him to shape the future of the team. He sees himself as a man of destiny: as in cricket, so in the wider game of Sri Lankan life.

STRAIGHT SHOOTER

Dean Jones

Dean Jones's sudden demise during the 2020 IPL season came like a sledgehammer blow. Filled with disbelief on seeing the news on TV, I called up some people I knew at the Star Sports network. Their affirmation sent me into deeper gloom. Cricket had lost a stalwart, and I had lost a dear friend.

Deano and I were of the same vintage. I had started a little earlier, but our careers more or less coincided, which meant running into each other often in the 1980s. Once we found common ground, we often shared thoughts on fellow players, from our own teams and others.

Our conversation wasn't limited to cricket. We talked of this, that, and everything under the sun – especially food. I take pride in the refinement of my palate and love a good meal, but Deano was a gourmand. He could discuss food in as much detail as he did cricket in his professorial bit for TV channels. Whenever he was in Mumbai, we would meet at my house or some restaurant of his choice. And vice versa when I was in Melbourne. One of my most memorable days Down Under was spending Christmas Day with Deano and his family (after we had retired). Not just the food, wine and occasion, it was the Jones's who made the day for us.

But it hadn't always been so hunky-dory. Deano and I were extremely competitive, and this showed in our early years in international cricket when India played Australia, and we clashed with each other on and off the field. Neither wanted to cede an inch. While the senior pros knew when to switch off, our battles would continue much longer. Some years later, when we had both settled down in international cricket, we genuinely warmed up to each other, and built an abiding friendship, based on mutual respect and trust that lasted till his unfortunate, premature death.

The turning point of sorts in our relationship was the Tied Test in 1986. We thought the Aussies would be easy to overcome on a slow turner in the heat and extreme humidity of Madras. Many overseas teams have come to grief in those conditions – in my time, as well as before and after. However, the match didn't pan out as we imagined because one Mr Dean Jones played the innings of a lifetime.

There were many heroes in that extraordinary contest, but the player with the most influence in the match was Deano, who made 210 runs in really tough conditions.

In the course of that innings, he puked, cursed and was close to tears for long periods, but always defiant. His double century was testimony to his character and determination. After he was dismissed, he had to be taken to hospital and put on a drip. But he gave his team the runs and captain Allan Border the confidence to make a terrific sporting declaration, enough to win a Test.

We took the challenge head on, and the result was a memorable tie, only the second in Test history. That match changed the mindset of a lot of young cricketers in that game, Deano and me included. His rise as a Test player of consequence started from here.

Deano was a flamboyant cricketer. His prowess as an ODI player was such that it tended to undermine his Test performances. But he was brilliant in the longest format too. How many players have averaged 46-plus after fifty-two Tests? He was one of the many pupils Allan Border mentored, but I'd venture that Deano was Allan's favourite for his vivacity and commitment. He was terrific both on and off the field.

Looking back, it seems strange that he was in and out of the Test team. I'd say it wasn't so much for lack of talent but because of his outspokenness, which is seldom appreciated by those in authority. That said, he was easily among the finest ODI players – not just in his era, but of all time – and never out of the Australian playing XI.

He had the strokes, the speed – when running between the wickets and fielding – and the daring to take on the opposition in the powerplay. Not just that, his thought process while batting in ODIs was ahead of most players of his era. He'd anticipate bowlers and pick up gaps in the field which other batsmen couldn't. He was a terrific all-round batsman, good against pace and spin, quick on his feet, never afraid of taking on the stiffest challenge. Along with Viv Richards and Javed Miandad, Deano was the best ODI batsman in the 1980s. Like

Miandad, Deano could get under the skin of the opposition. Sometimes, this boomeranged, like when he asked Curtly Ambrose to take off his wristband for no particular reason and Australia had to pay the price for it. I don't know what his teammates told him after that Ambrose demolition act, but it couldn't have been pleasant.

However, Deano was his own man and could ruffle a few feathers, as player and later as commentator. This got him into a spot of bother at times. While he could be indiscreet, I'll vouch that he was never mean or malicious. We spent a lot of time together in Singapore, working for ESPN, and I always found him to be fair. His knowledge of the game, its history, and his reading of match situations was excellent. We had our differences on issues, but nothing that couldn't be resolved over a pint of beer.

Deano wasn't dogmatic. Cricket for him was not just livelihood, but life. He was always thinking ahead, always young at heart. Such a tragedy to see him leave the field so early.

DAREDEVIL

Aravinda De Silva

Aravinda De Silva was the ultimate big-match player. I've seen many very good players get jittery and lose their nerve when the stakes are high. With Aravinda, it was the other way around. He got easily bored in run-of-the-mill contests, but would be a batsman transformed when the demands were tougher.

His magnificent contribution in Sri Lanka's 1996 World Cup victory stands testimony to this quality – particularly the way he batted against India in the semi-final and Australia in the final, the two strongest teams in the tournament.

In the emotion-charged semi-final against India at Kolkata, he came in to bat when Sri Lanka were rocked by Javagal Srinath who had taken 2 wickets in his very first over. The situation at that stage, if not suggesting hopelessness, called for a measured approach at the very least. Instead, Aravinda decided to dominate this psychologically crucial phase by taking the attack to the Indian bowlers. And how!

He made 60-odd runs, which was worth more than a century in the context of the match. His masterly batting tamed both pace and spin, loosened India's vice-like grip on the match, and gave his own bowlers a fighting total to defend. As it turned out, on a rapidly wearing pitch, India went into terminal decline once Sachin fell, and Sri Lanka won with plenty to spare.

The venue of the World Cup final was Lahore and Sri Lanka's opponents were Australia. This was a grudge match, for the two countries had clashed more than once on the field – and several times off it – through strong statements against each other on the issue of Muttiah Muralitharan's bowling action. Though the match was being played in the subcontinent, Australia were clear favourites because of the quality and experience of their line-up which boasted Mark Taylor, the Waugh twins, Ricky Ponting, Michael Bevan, Glenn McGrath and Shane Warne, who had hit top form.

I was among those calling the final on TV. Australia scored a modest 241, but most of us in the commentary box believed this was good enough to quell Sri Lanka, given the pressures of a final and the presence of Warne to exploit a slowish track. As in the semis, Sri Lanka lost 2 quick wickets again, but Aravinda came up with a masterclass century, not only salvaging the innings but leading the run charge in such commanding style that one could almost see the Aussies waving the white handkerchief.

This was a vastly different Aravinda from the one I had first seen in 1985 when we toured Sri Lanka. He made his Test debut against us as a nineteen-year-old in the first match at Colombo, and we got some idea of his prowess when he hit Kapil Dev for a couple of sixes in his first over as Sri Lanka tried to chase an impossible target in the second innings.

Aravinda's daredevilry had got our dressing room talking, though only briefly because he was not our main threat. This came from seasoned batsmen Duleep Mendis, Roy Dias and Ranjan Madugalle, and pace bowlers Rumesh Ratnayake, Ashantha de Mel and Saliya Ahangama.

I kept track of Aravinda's career because he was not only a very organized batsman, but also an attractive one. In his early years it had seemed he was more interested in having a blast, being a show pony. But as he matured – and I think his captain Arjuna Ranatunga had some role to play in it – he controlled his aggression without compromising, taking toll of run-scoring deliveries. County stints with Kent also helped him value his wicket and runs.

Over a period of time, Aravinda grew into a superb all-round, all-wicket batsman, always attractive to watch. His repertoire of strokes was full to the brim. My favourite was the cover drive, played on the up off the back foot. Only Sachin, among those I've seen, played this stroke better.

We've had an enduring friendship for almost four decades. A warm man, and a great host, Aravinda is the man I call first when in Sri Lanka.

WAZ TO MY SHAZ

Wasim Akram

Although Malcolm Marshall was the best fast bowler I've ever played, Wasim Akram comes a close second. I consider him a 'freak' for I have seen none other with the same talent or variety as Wasim at his best.

He could bowl from over or round the wicket without losing even the slightest control. Adapting swiftly to a different line is not easy, especially for a pace bowler, which shows how much quality time Wasim spent in the nets to master this.

He also had the widest range of deliveries among the fast bowlers I've played or seen. He could bowl really fast, or cut down pace to almost slow medium, but what made him especially dangerous was late swing and reverse swing – particularly the latter, which he would use cleverly to bamboozle even well-set batsmen.

Reverse swing is possible when the shine on one side of the ball is maintained by constant polishing. Making some nicks and dents on the other side and picking the seam also helps, provided of course you don't get caught. In the past, bowlers could get away with this rather easily, but with TV cameras now catching every bit of the action, there is serious threat of being caught and penalized.

When I was playing, Pakistanis were masters at 'preparing' a ball for reverse swing. Imran Khan was its finest exponent in the 1980s. Imran had learnt the craft from Sarfraz Nawaz, who was nearing the end of his career when India played Pakistan in 1982-83, but was still wily and dangerous.

It was from these two that Wasim imbibed the best lessons in reverse swing. In fact, he went a couple of notches higher in skill. Being a left-arm bowler made it that much more difficult for right-hand batsmen to read him, but it was his genius in all conditions that makes Wasim arguably the best left-arm pacer ever.

A hefty guy with large hands, he used this to his advantage by changing his grip on the ball for different deliveries. I don't think he left even a centimetre of leather or seam left unexplored to improvise.

Wasim's bowling style was somewhat unorthodox. He didn't have a big final leap as most fast bowlers do. Rather, he steamed in and delivered the ball with a whippy action, putting a lot of shoulder and back into it, surprising batsmen with the pace or bounce he could get off even a short run up.

He used the crease superbly too, and his ability to use a new or old ball equally well posed serious problems for any batsman. He was one bowler who didn't need a pitch or conditions to make him effective. In all the years I've played and watched cricket, I can think of only two bowlers who were not stymied by an unhelpful pitch. Macko was one, Wasim the other.

He was mentally very tough too, and a challenge always spurred him on. When we toured Pakistan in 1989, Wasim was struggling a bit with a dodgy groin. We thought, 'Chalo, it's one less stress for our batting unit.' But he came back stronger and faster in each spell, picking up crucial wickets.

In limited-overs cricket, his accuracy and control over late swing and yorkers made him the most difficult bowler to play in his time. The shorter version of the game demands constant improvisations like cross-seam grip, variations in pace, slow and quick bouncers, etc. And in this, Wasim was way ahead of his contemporaries. He could catch batsmen completely unawares, as we saw in the 1992 World Cup final where his two wickets off successive deliveries turned the match in Pakistan's favour.

I have a great personal equation with Wasim. He's a terrific bloke, easy-going, hassle-free, and loves the good things in life – which is how I see myself too. For all his achievements, he's incredibly modest about his stature in the game.

I had several years playing hard cricket against him and he was always looking to hit my stumps, head or toes! He never gave an inch. But post-retirement, when we did commentary together, we found a chemistry that made all our contests in the middle something to enjoy rather than remember with bitterness.

For the decade or so that we shared the commentary box together, I had more fun with him than anybody else. The *Shaz & Waz Show*, put together by ESPN Star Sports in the breaks during matches, became so popular largely because of the spontaneity in our exchanges. There was little that was predetermined apart from the instruction that there should be a lot of banter and fun. That was easy as we got along like a house on fire, often ending up on the same side of a debate as our thoughts on cricket and life are so alike.

TOUGH COOKIE

Steve Waugh

Steve Waugh, a few years my junior in both age and cricketing vintage, was one of the toughest blokes I encountered on the field. In a long and distinguished career, he performed far above what most people thought he would, simply because he was mentally so tough.

Like his first captain, Allan Border, Steve's determination and willingness to go to any length to succeed were his biggest assets. He had a never-say-die attitude and wore his ambition on his sleeve, uncaring about what anyone else thought.

I played a lot against Steve, not just in international cricket, but also in the English county circuit where he was a pro for Somerset. We were both young then, and I found him to be a hardcore competitor. He would mutter things under his breath at rivals even then, hoping verbal volleys would distract them.

He kept up the sledging throughout his career, but, like most Aussie cricketers, didn't carry grudges beyond the field.

He was not as outgoing with opponents as the late Dean Jones, also part of the young brigade nursed by Border into international eminence. Deano would readily spend time in the opponents' dressing room after a day's play. Steve was reserved and would open up only with a few. Many cricketers on the circuit found him aloof and self-absorbed. I found him easy to talk to once the ice was broken when we were playing county cricket. Perhaps this was because we belonged to the same age group. Also, playing as an overseas pro has challenges, and sharing experiences was of mutual benefit.

My introduction to Steve had come before I began playing county cricket. It was on my first tour to Australia in 1986 that I heard about the Waugh twins, Steve and Mark, who were being spoken of very highly in cricket circles Down Under. The Waugh brothers, in fact, were being compared to the Chappell brothers. Those were mighty boots to fill. The contribution of Ian and Greg Chappell to Australian cricket would fill up a library. Not unexpectedly, there was a fair amount of scepticism about Steve and Mark too.

In his debut Test, against us at Melbourne in 1985, Steve couldn't make an impact. He fell victim to Laxman Sivaramakrishnan's delivery in the first innings for 13 and, in the second, I bowled him round his legs for 5. I recall his bewildered look after the ball hit the stumps. But he recovered his composure quickly, and walked off with a steely expression to suggest there would be days when he would get my better.

Not every young cricketer, however talented, can succeed or sustain initial success at the highest level. To survive a long career, requires grit, determination and ambition in huge measure. That Steve went on to play for almost a decade and a half after that shows mental toughness and strength of character to succeed.

Steve came into his own in the 1987 World Cup as an all-rounder. Mentored by Border, who had played often enough in the subcontinent to know the pitches and conditions, he became a foil to the fast bowlers, bowling medium-paced cutters with immaculate control, so much so that he was used by Border in the death overs. He made an impact with bat and ball in the two league matches we played, though his best performance was against Pakistan in the semi-final, where his gutsy, aggressive hitting in the end overs proved to be the difference between the two teams.

The next big step was in succeeding as a batsman in England. Coping with swing and seam movement, sometimes for two or three days, is the stiffest test for overseas batsmen. It's in contrast to the conditions in Australia, where pitches have more bounce, though not so much lateral movement. Runs didn't come to him on a platter. He had to work hard on technical adjustments for the softer English pitches, but over time he established himself as the most reliable, if not the best, batsman in those conditions.

Waugh's captaincy record is quite remarkable. By the time Mark Taylor retired, the Aussies were the best side in the world. But even the best set of players needs to be held together by a strong man at the top. Steve was not the most liked in his own team, but became one of the most successful captains, which reflects well as much on the Aussie ethos as his own leadership abilities. His personal batting form ensured there would be no upheavals.

Not as naturally gifted as his twin, Mark, Steve made up for it with fierce determination. Mark's biggest asset was his wonderful hands, in batting and fielding; Steve's was mental toughness. In a crisis, his resolve to succeed would get even stronger. If I have to pay money to watch, it would be for Mark, but if I have to depend on someone to save my life, I'd pick Steve.

FAST FRIENDS

Curtly Ambrose and Courtney Walsh

Of the eleven Test centuries I've scored, the one which gave me most satisfaction was the 107 against West Indies at Barbados in 1989. It nudges ahead of my maiden century against Pakistan in 1982-83 and the double century against Australia at Sydney in 1991-92 simply for the challenges involved. The Kensington Oval in those days was still fiery, the raucous crowd was braying for our heads while we battled to put up a decent score in the second innings against an attack that boasted Malcolm Marshall, Ian Bishop, Curtly Ambrose and Courtney Walsh. I have never felt so intimidated while batting.

Macko, of course, was the best fast bowler I've played. He was in his element on his home ground, and being egged on by hysterical fans to go past Lance Gibbs's record of 309 wickets. Ian Bishop was the quickest among West Indies' fast bowlers then, a strapping young man who bowled excellent lines and a superb outswinger. It's a pity that his career ended prematurely because of injury for he looked destined to become an all-time great, following in the footsteps of Andy Roberts, Michael. Holding, Joel Garner and Macko. Like this great quartet, he had a quiet demeanour on the field, and a mean hunger for wickets.

Walsh and Ambrose were relative newcomers. Hailing from Jamaica, Walsh was touted as successor to the great Michael Holding. He was tall, athletic and his run up, if not as silken as Holding's, was smooth and pleasing to the eye. He had made his debut in 1984 and, with the old guard barring Macko fading away, was just about coming into his own. Ambrose was from Antigua like Andy Roberts. He was a rookie, having debuted only a season earlier. He was very dissimilar to Roberts in physique and bowling style: skyscraper tall, not genuinely quick but fast-medium and not reputed to be very hostile.

The thinking in our dressing room was that if we could see off Macko and Bishop, we would have a fair chance in the match. Our thinking was wrong. Though Bishop took 6 wickets in our first innings and Macko took 5 in the second, Walsh and Ambrose kept things so tight when the two main wicket-takers were off the attack that we had no respite.

To score substantial runs against the West Indies in those days, you had to steel yourself to bat four or five hours. These guys gave nothing for free. Batting for so long involved taking some blows on the body, arms, etc. I batted for more than four hours for the century, but I can't remember a single loose delivery from either bowler. I played most deliveries off my chest, and they weren't even bowling short!

We could score only 251 in the second innings; West Indies won by eight wickets to take the lead in the series, which they eventually won 3–0. By that time, both these bowlers had ensured their places in the Test team. Within a year or so, they had become the leading bowlers for the West Indies. When they retired, Ambrose and Walsh were regarded as among the best fast-bowling pairs in the history of the game.

Looking back, I'd say they rank among the top ten of all time for their economy and strike rate, and the number of wickets they took and matches they won. They were a study in contrast as fast bowlers, but together made a tough pair to face.

Ambrose could drop the ball on a penny anywhere in the world – such was his accuracy, control and ability to adjust length swiftly. He had a smooth run up, but his great height enabled him to get tremendous bounce from any pitch. This was the key to his success. He gave batsmen no leeway, forcing them into mistakes whenever they tried something adventurous. After all, you can't remain runless for eternity. And even if your defence was rock solid, an unplayable delivery would be just around the corner.

Ambrose was an enigma, calm and phlegmatic even during a torrid spell, hardly betraying any emotion. He would go about his job like a thorough professional, but if you rattled him and if he got angry there was a heavy price to pay – as the late Dean Jones, and even the English team, realized on several occasions. A riled-up Ambrose would blow like a typhoon. Remember the match against Australia at Perth when he took 7 wickets for 1 run in a spell? If a bowler has this kind of ability, to pick up 5–7 wickets in a few overs, my advice to the prudent is to not provoke him.

All told, Ambrose was a champion fast bowler, an unsmiling assassin always preying on batsmen, sometimes on a short fuse. Who would have thought that after retiring, he would become a guitarist in a rock band and play in nightclubs in Antigua! An iconoclast if ever there was one!

Courtney Walsh walks into the Hall of Fame for the number of wickets he's taken as well as the sheer longevity of his career. He was an outstanding bowler who absorbed the pressure of bowling a humongous number of overs all over the world without ever losing his cool. At most, you'd see an eyebrow go up, as if perplexed at the unfairness of a situation.

With over 500 wickets, Walsh – the first bowler to get past the milestone – occupies a special place in the pantheon of bowling greats. He was unlike most of the other West Indies fast bowlers I played. They were all wicket-takers used in short bursts, but Walsh was a workhorse; he never tired. Because the supply of fine West Indies fast bowlers had dwindled somewhat by then, Walsh actually did the work of two. This was most admirable. Even in conditions which gave little help, he kept coming at you, over after over with consistent pace and hostility, not saving himself an ounce of energy, not ceding an inch to the batsman.

He could surprise batsmen on any surface. They might think that he was slackening just a little bit, when, suddenly, he would surprise them with a delivery that erupted from just short of a length. I've been at the receiving end a fair number of times. My counsel to myself and my batting partners was always, 'Watch out for this guy when he looks the most spent.'

Above all, Walsh deserves credit for captaining the West Indies team with distinction. He was a great ambassador for the game too, and his choosing to not run out Saleem Jaffar in the 1987 World Cup is testimony to how he saw and played the game.

Walsh and Ambrose were the last great pair of West Indies fast bowlers. Hopefully, a new generation will take the helm soon, for losing both players almost simultaneously cost the team heavily. In a way, this was also Brian Lara's bad luck. Imagine if these two had been around with Brian in full form!

Walsh and Ambrose were a splendid pair of bowlers and good friends too. I was keen to catch up with them when we toured the West Indies in 2019. Walsh came over for a drink and we reminisced about old times over a few pints. Ambrose was held up somewhere else and couldn't make it, but I hope to held up with him one of these days, and show him a few spots on my arms and ribs where I was hit by the pair of them. The bruises have gone, but the memory exists.

HEART-THROB OF A BILLION

Sachin Tendulkar

Sachin Tendulkar enjoys Don Bradman-like stature in the game. I'd say probably greater in terms of influence, given that the times he played in saw the cricket universe expanding to numerous countries and becoming a multibillion-dollar industry.

Apart from making Indian cricket strong, relevant and lucrative, Sachin was the most talismanic player and biggest ambassador internationally in this period of growth. His batting exploits and his endearing persona made him cricket's biggest draw. The BCCI certainly had to expand the dimensions of its coffers because of his enormous appeal!

A player's mettle is determined not by runs and centuries they make in a brief productive phase, but longevity of career. Cricket history is replete with those who hit a purple patch for a few years but couldn't sustain at the same level thereafter. The truly great have the remarkable ability to maintain a high level of excellence for a decade or more, with very few troughs.

Sachin's international career was monumental, lasting twenty-four years. I am loath to compare him with former greats who had similar tenures in international cricket – certainly not Bradman, who undoubtedly represents the pinnacle of batsmanship. Different eras throw up different challenges, and players should be assessed accordingly. Modern batsmen have a couple of distinct advantages in that they don't have to play on uncovered pitches and have fantastic protective gear, without which their struggle would be greater. On the other hand, their predecessors didn't have to prove themselves in different formats, which requires versatility in skills, or travel to so many countries so often, and therefore, adapt and adjust to different conditions.

All things considered, sustained excellence comes only to a few. Sachin stands at the very top in this exclusive cluster. Add to this the persistent and humungous pressure of the expectations of a billion-plus obsessive fans, and his batting exploits acquire an extraordinary dimension. Indians adore their cricket heroes, but are also unforgiving to those who fail to meet their expectations. Sachin was unfazed by this onus and hardly ever failed in his long career, which is mind-boggling.

He seemed special from the time I first saw him. Prolific run-scoring as a schoolboy got him into the headlines. Word travels fast on the Bombay cricket circuit and I was eager to see first-hand how good Sachin was. What I saw impressed me immediately. He had so much time to play shots. He was making tall scores too, which reflected both appetite and aptitude.

He made his Test debut in Pakistan in 1989 when only sixteen. When most boys are still growing physically and tackling teenage troubles, Sachin was battling against Imran Khan, Wasim Akram and Waqar Younis with considerable skill and, more importantly, a big heart. In the team, we were all excited about the youngster's talent, and also curious to see how he would fare at the highest level. Not every promising youngster goes on to become a successful cricketer. Progress from the junior to senior level comes with many hurdles, the main one being self-doubt.

However, I don't think self-doubt featured in Sachin's mind at all. He exuded confidence from day one and was an eager learner, wanting to get better and better with every match. Early on the tour, he came and asked me if he was being too hasty in playing shots. Perhaps a tad too much was my sense, for he wanted to dominate bowlers as soon as he came in. My advice to him was to always be positive, but understand conditions and bowlers first, give them respect till you have got your eye in, and then take over. He finished the Pakistan tour with two Test half-centuries.

Less than a year later, he saved us a Test match at Old Trafford with fine technical skills and a steely temperament. His ability to absorb pressure and hardship without flinching was remarkable, especially at that stage in his career. It was against Australia in 1991-92, though, that Sachin took giant steps towards becoming the master batsman everybody now acknowledges.

Watching him from 22 yards away as we put up a partnership of just under 200 at the Sydney Cricket Ground in the 1991-92 Test, I realized how enormously gifted he was. His technique was purer than anything I'd seen in somebody so young. Everything was out of a coaching manual, or better.

He had a strong streak of defiance in him then. I was having a constant powwow with the Aussie bowlers while getting to my double century and was actually enjoying their needling because it only made me more determined. Soon, Sachin was also being targeted. 'Don't worry, I'll also give it to them,' he told me matter-of-factly in Marathi.

I told him not to bother, to just concentrate and ignore the distraction. He did that, raising the bar even higher as he hit Merv Hughes and Craig McDermott with power and precision. Once Allan Border and Co. realized the sledging was actually having the opposite effect on the youngster, it quickly stopped.

In the last Test of the series, we suffered a massive defeat on a fiery Perth pitch, but Sachin's masterful 114 in the first innings became the highlight of the match. The manner in which he flayed the strong Aussie attack, rising on his toes for back foot cover drives or cuts belied his relative inexperience and revealed his class.

I rate it as among the top three of his fifty-one Test hundreds. After that innings, he made the number four spot in the Indian batting order his very own. Within only a couple of years in international cricket, Sachin had made an indelible impact on the game. The question now was not whether he was as good as his early potential suggested, but how far he would go?

I won't go into details of his career as these are widely known. The quality of his batsmanship was superb. Technically, I would rate him Gavaskar's equal among all the batsmen I've seen: an almost impenetrable defence, impeccable judgement of line and length, strong off front foot and back, decisive in his footwork, possessing every stroke in the book, knowing which ball to hit, and consistency in run-scoring wherever he played. Add to that a fantastically composed mind that could not be flustered easily; in fact, it fed on challenges. In limited-overs cricket, he showed a keen sense for improvisation to go with classical, orthodox batting. I think playing as an opener in ODIs helped Sachin immensely even in Tests. It kept his reflexes sharp and was instrumental in him playing for so long.

The race for batting honours with the likes of Brian Lara, Ricky Ponting, Rahul Dravid, Jacques Kallis, Inzamam-ul-Haq and Kevin Pietersen, among others, kept his competitive juices flowing and enriched the game.

My career ended in 1994 and I shifted quickly into the broadcast universe after meeting Mark Mascarenhas of WorldTel, who I then introduced to Sachin. I'm glad Mark had the vision to take charge of the young player's career. He was like a father figure to Sachin, and saw in his talent and mass appeal a way to make cricket grow exponentially. Unfortunately, Mark died in a car accident in early 2002. But the brief partnership between him and Sachin had gone a long way in redefining Indian cricket.

Sachin's career reads like a fairy tale. He hardly put a foot wrong from his teens till he retired at forty. He was masterly with the bat, and dignified in whatever he did on and off the field. To remain controversy-free for over twenty-five years in the public eye is impossible to imagine, especially amidst the noise and din of Indian cricket.

Because runs and centuries appeared to come so easily to him, the hard effort – physical and mental – behind them is often glossed over. But anybody who's played the game at the highest level will tell you that nothing comes as a freebie; everything has to be earned.

Six attempts at the World Cup are proof of Sachin's perseverance. So many great players have never seen a World Cup title. He never gave up and was finally rewarded when India won the title in 2011. By the time he retired a couple of seasons later, Sachin had all the batting records one could think of.

Pint-sized in physical stature, but a colossus all the same.

THUNDERBOLT UNLEASHED

Waqar Younis

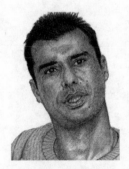

Fast bowlers are most dangerous when they hunt in pairs. The West Indies in the 1980s went a step ahead and used a four-man pace attack that earned them unchecked success. But this was an aberration. To have so many bowlers of similar wicket-taking quality in all conditions is an act of fortune.

Generally, if a team has even two incisive fast bowlers – and a spinner or two in support – it will win more matches than lose. Ray Lindwall–Keith Miller, Fred Trueman–Brian Statham, Dennis Lillee–Jeff Thomson and, in recent times, James Anderson–Stuart Broad are some of the great pairs that have made a huge difference to the results of the matches they've played in. They've also made fast bowling thrilling to watch, though the batsmen who faced these bowlers would not have felt as enthusiastic.

I've held back one pair from the list above; I can't make up my mind if this wasn't the most destructive combination ever. Since there's no yardstick by which an answer to this can be found, I'll take the easy way out: in my time, there was no deadlier duo than Wasim Akram and Waqar Younis.

I've already mentioned how Wasim was the best fast bowler I had faced after Malcolm Marshall. In the cluster of great fast bowlers, Waqar isn't too far behind either. When the two bowled from opposite ends, it was a furious assault of pace, swing, yorkers and bouncers that left little scope for batsmen to escape.

I remember one match, in particular, between Pakistan and England at the Oval in 1992. Even on TV, their bowling was breathtaking. Wasim cleaned up the England batting in the first innings, taking 6 wickets, while Waqar blew away the top order in the second innings in which he took 5 wickets. Between them, they took 15 wickets in the match; England lost by 10 wickets.

In this partnership, Waqar was not a foil to Wasim but an equal. In fact, for the first few years after they came together, he was perhaps feared more because of his greater pace and hostility, which began with his long, sprinting – and somewhat menacing – run up. Firing thunderbolts with late swing that crushed the toes and souls of batsmen, Waqar was often unplayable at his peak in the 1990s. Again, because he was essentially a swing bowler, his success was not dependent on the pitch.

Waqar made his Test debut against us at Karachi, the same match in which Sachin Tendulkar too made his entry into international cricket. There was a great deal of interest around these two young players who had already built a reputation for themselves.

Imran Khan, always on the lookout for new talent, had fast-tracked Waqar into the Pakistan team and there was a buzz when the young bowler took the field for the first Test. The entire Indian team was in the porch of the dressing room to see him take the new ball because of what we had heard about him.

Waqar was tearaway quickie then and picked up four wickets in the first innings, but he didn't yet have the same control or swing that was to make him so dreaded a few years later. With Imran as mentor and Wasim as colleague, he improved by leaps and bounds.

While both could work up furious pace – Waqar more so when he was younger, and Wasim almost throughout his career – they were of contrasting styles, and not just because one bowled left-handed and the other right. Wasim was more slippery because of his action, which camouflaged the ball, not allowing the batsman to read what delivery might come up next. He had a quick arm action, was a master of late movement either way and his bouncers were vicious.

Waqar was nastily fast, steaming in off a long run up, every stride adding to his aggression. He had a slightly round-arm action, which made his short-pitched deliveries less dangerous than Wasim's. His forte was pitching a fullish length, allowing optimum scope for late movement. The pace at which Waqar bowled also meant that batsmen, perforce, had to make a very late call on how to play the swing. At his peak, he was probably the greatest exponent of inswing. His ability to curve the ball in late, like a hissing snake, was unbelievable and left in its wake many a shattered stump and tattered reputation.

When in full flight, a great sight, best seen batting from the other end or, even better, from the safety of the dressing room.

TWINKLING FOOTWORK, DAZZLING STROKES

Brian Lara

 Brian Lara and Sachin Tendulkar were the two best batsmen of their generation. This has been said so often as to have become a cliché, but it's true. I followed their entire careers, as a fellow player initially and then as a commentator – and believe me, it is very, very tough to choose between the two.

Being contemporaries helped both batsmen as they fed off each other's achievements, and inspired each other to greater heights. This also helped cricket become a bigger spectacle and expanded the fan base for the sport worldwide. Both had immense pride in their own ability, and the race for batting supremacy produced many thrilling moments and memorable knocks. Even when they were playing other opponents, the Sachin v Lara rivalry never ceased.

While both were geniuses with the bat and notched up those several thousand runs each, Sachin and Lara had some key dissimilarities. One was right-handed, the other left-handed. Sachin was immersed in classically orthodox technique, punctuated with amazing improvisations in limited-overs cricket, whereas Lara was bursting with exotic Caribbean flair that always set the pulse racing in any format.

I'll cease the comparison here and focus on Lara, who not only lived up to the wonderful legacy of West Indies stroke players, but left his own mark to match that of the likes Frank Worrell, Everton Weekes and Clyde Walcott, Gary Sobers, Rohan Kanhai, Viv Richards, Gordon Greenidge and Clive Lloyd.

Lara first caught my eye in 1989 when we were touring the West Indies. He was playing for the Under-23 team and made 182 sparkling runs against us at St. Kitts island. Yet, I can't recall him hitting one ball in the air! Despite being so young, his use of feet to our spinners was incredible, especially so since our attack included leg spinner Narendra Hirwani, who had taken 16 wickets on his Test debut just the previous season, and off-spinners Arshad Ayub and M. Venkataramana.

Belying his inexperience, Lara treated them all with utter disdain, almost as if this was some friendly club-level match. I wasn't in the playing XI, but I didn't miss a single minute of his knock, so compelling, such a joy he was to watch.

Even at that early stage in his career, his genius was evident in his strokes. Lara's flowing drives came with a high backlift and an equally flamboyant follow up, the cuts were fierce and timed to perfection, and he pulled with quicksilver footwork to get into the right position. We were all surprised when he couldn't break into the West Indies team in that series.

Lara seldom needed to hit the ball in the air to score at a rapid pace. He mitigated the risk element, but was supremely adept at picking gaps in the field – which explains why he could make such tall scores throughout his career. His splendid timing would send the ball to the fence 'like a tracer bullet', to use my favourite phrase. In his Test career, he did employ the lofted stroke frequently, but judiciously, ensuring he cleared the fence or the field when he did so.

Though he made thousands of runs against pace, the hallmark of Lara's batsmanship for me was how he played spin. One normally expects West Indian batsmen to be masters against fast bowling, but this guy was a maestro against slow bowlers on difficult pitches in their own den. I haven't seen anybody play slow bowling better.

He would dance down the track with twinkling footwork, taking swift and precise steps to the pitch of the ball, in defence or attack. Being a naturally attacking batsman, more often than not, it was the latter. That he scored more than 600 runs against Muttiah Muralitharan at his peak in Sri Lanka in 2001 is testimony to Lara's prowess against spin even on pitches that afforded sharp turn. No other batsman has scored as many runs in three Tests anywhere in the subcontinent. Murali took 24 wickets in that series, which puts Lara's 'one-man show' into perspective.

On his day, Lara was a spectator's delight and an opponent's nightmare because he would be impossible to contain. In fact, Lara posed a serious challenge to commentators too, because he could exhaust your vocabulary, phrases and imagery soon after taking to the field.

Look at those Himalayan scores: 501 not out, 400 not out, 375, nine double centuries, two triple centuries … Gosh!

A true-blue genius. Enough said.

SUPREME SOLOIST

Sanath Jayasuriya

 Sanath Jayasuriya transformed the face of one-day cricket batting during the 1996 World Cup. He was a brilliant stroke player and several of his innings were breathtaking. I've been on air on quite a few occasions when he's batted, struggling to find words which would adequately describe the tenor of his innings as he went about slamming fours and sixes with complete disdain.

One such knock was against Pakistan in Singapore in 1996. Jayasuriya took the bowling – which included Wasim Akram, Waqar Younis and Shoaib Akhtar – to the cleaners, getting his century in just 48 balls! In the 2003 World Cup, we would see something similar when Sachin Tendulkar and Virender Sehwag turned the heat on these bowlers. However, Sachin and Viru were world renowned for their stroke play. In 1996, Jayasuriya hardly commanded the same attention, and his furious, world-record-setting innings took everyone by surprise.

Jayasuriya's record was broken by fifteen-year-old Shahid Afridi a mere seven months later as Pakistan exacted revenge on the Sri Lankans for the trauma in Singapore. Sandwiched in between these centuries was the World Cup, which brought Sri Lanka its highest cricketing accolade, and Jayasuriya into the limelight.

The Singapore century was to be the precursor to his supercharged batting in the World Cup. Martin Crowe had innovated with a pinch-hitting opener in the 1992 World Cup. In a stunning masterstroke, captain Arjuna Ranatunga opened with two in 1996.

Small-made wicketkeeper Romesh Kaluwitharana, who batted right-hand, joined the left-handed Jayasuriya in a move which surprised many, including me. Ranatunga was taking a big risk. But over the next few weeks, as the opening pair created pandemonium with their unrestrained, aggressive batting, it became clear that the captain knew what he was doing. He had worked it out correctly that the subcontinental pitches in the 1996 World Cup would be batsmen-friendly, even in pace and bounce, and full of runs. Moreover, the white ball, now in use in ODIs, did not get quite the same movement, which mitigated the risk of extravagant stroke play.

More than technical ability and stuff, however, what matters in such situations is the captain's faith. Ranatunga did not give Jayasuriya and Kaluwitharana the licence to fail; rather, he gave them the confidence to succeed. Together they powered through some of the best bowling attacks in the world and helped Sri Lanka notch up a spectacular World Cup win.

At his best, Jayasuriya was virtually impossible to contain. Strong forearms helped him get strength from a shortish backlift, and tough wrists gave the ball direction to beat the field. Since he had a penchant for playing lofted shots, fielders, more often than not, became superfluous. He was brutal with his cuts, pulls and hooks, latching on to even the smallest mistake in length or line with explosive strokes, the sounds of which would resonate round the stadium and leave bowlers crestfallen.

From the 1996 World Cup, Jayasuriya went from strength to strength. He lost Kalu as a partner, but found a niche for himself as a supreme soloist, able to win matches off his own bat, and sometimes with the ball too. Again, strong fingers to complement powerful arms, shoulders and wrists, helped him get the ball to rip and bounce off pitches where other spinners occasionally struggled.

He wasn't only a limited-overs specialist: fourteen Test centuries, including a mammoth 340 against India, show how good he could be in the longest format too. But he was at his most dangerous and exhilarating best in the shorter formats. A match-winner who helped his country rise to the top.

SUPER HIT

Inzamam-ul-Haq

Inzamam-ul-Haq was my favourite for post-match presentations. He would feature often as Man of the Match, and even more regularly as Pakistan's captain. Early in his career, he would sidle up to me before the presentations began and whisper, 'Please ask me questions in Urdu or Hindi, keep English to a minimum.'

'I'll try, but my Urdu and Hindi are not as good yours, so I may have difficulty,' was my response. We both agreed to play it by ear and use whichever language was easy for us in the situation. I don't know if our interactions improved his English or my Urdu, and what listeners made of them, but they were always a lot of fun.

Inzy didn't fancy attention. Post-match formalities were a chore for him, at least in his initial years – mainly because he was a shy guy, most comfortable with close friends and in the dressing room. But he had a sense of humour, and from what I gathered from Wasim Akram, Rameez Raja and some others who played with him, he could be quite wicked!

On the field, however, he had no compunction at all; his shyness disappeared completely. Cricket came to him naturally, and he loved batting. In my estimation, Inzy was among the best of his era. When batsmen of the 1990s and the first decade of this century are discussed, the names that usually figure at the top are Sachin Tendulkar, Brian Lara, Ricky Ponting and Jacques Kallis. I'll add a fifth: Inzamam-ul-Haq.

He arrived on the international cricket stage in style during the 1992 World Cup. My own stint in the tournament was short-lived as I got injured very early and had to return home. I had heard that Pakistan had brought some talented youngsters to Australia, but there was hardly any mention of Inzy till his blazing knock in the semi-final which kayoed a high-flying New Zealand.

I saw him on TV, in his early twenties, packing amazing punch in his strokes as he played all round the wicket. He wasn't heavily built then, and there was more timing than strength, which carried the ball to the boundary. What caught my eye even then was his balance, playing off front or back foot. Not easy for a youngster on the seaming tracks in New Zealand or the bouncier pitches of Australia.

His stroke of luck was Imran Khan spotting him pulling Wasim and Waqar Younis in the nets with nonchalant ease. Imran was always on the lookout for potential match-winners. He would go by his gut, use his clout to fast-track them into the national side, then back them to the hilt. Some gambles didn't pay off. Others like Waqar and Inzy became superhits. In Inzy's case, though, it must be remembered that Imran didn't play after the 1992 World Cup, so he did not have a benevolent senior looking after him. He had to follow up on his World Cup success with more success, especially in Test cricket, still the dominant format of the game then – and, not surprisingly, he did.

While his ODI record is fantastic too, it is Inzy's Test match batting that made him a modern great. Within no time after the 1992 World Cup, Inzy showed excellence across formats, and a deep ambition for scoring runs in Test cricket. A good grounding in technique enabled him to adopt a wide range of strokes, and with experience, he built up a rock steady temperament and put a heavy premium on his wicket. His great strength was the time he had to play, especially fast bowling, and more particularly, the hook and pull shots. These strokes carry a lot of risk unless the batsman gets in position quickly to be on top of the ball. Mishits and top edges are common from batsmen with sluggish footwork.

As his career progressed, Inzy became a batsman who could hold an innings together, and dazzle with aggressive stroke play, depending on the situation. In this period, Pakistan also had two other fine batsman, Younis Khan and Mohammad Yousuf, but the pivotal player was undoubtedly Inzy. Like Javed Miandad, he could score in all conditions against any attack. But unlike Miandad, who could make batting look grotesque (though he was always effective!), Inzy had finesse, style and panache. He never looked impatient or flustered even when the bowling was on top. When in form, he was wonderful to watch.

Within a couple of years of his debut in 1992, Inzy filled out, which made him the butt of jokes. Of gentle demeanour, he cared little for what anybody said. Like Arjuna Ranatunga, he made the game go at his pace. Nothing could hurry him up. His running between wickets caught the attention of critics and, while sometimes comical to see, it rarely cost him his wicket. In any case, Inzy was such a mighty stroke player that it was the fielders who were doing most of the running anyway. But one day in Toronto, the taunting got out of control, and he lost his cool. He jumped over the fence in a flash and, bat in hand, chased his tormentor a fair distance before he was stopped!

I was at that match, in the commentary box. I've never seen Inzy run – nor anybody run *away* from him – faster. It was some sight and showed a side of his character which nobody had seen, for otherwise there was no player as phlegmatic as him in the game.

HE MADE FIELDING SEXY

Jonty Rhodes

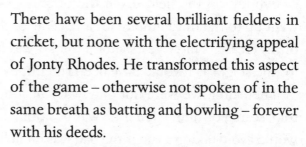 There have been several brilliant fielders in cricket, but none with the electrifying appeal of Jonty Rhodes. He transformed this aspect of the game – otherwise not spoken of in the same breath as batting and bowling – forever with his deeds.

Jonty made fielding sexy and spectacular. He came to prominence in the 1991-92 World Cup when he ran out Inzamam-ul-Haq with a direct hit while still airborne. South Africa did not win the Cup, did not even reach the final, but Inzy's run-out became the abiding image of the tournament.

After making a huge impact in the World Cup, Jonty announced himself in the Test arena with another sensational effort, of which I have first-hand experience. India's first Test in the 1993 series against South Africa was at Durban. The third umpire was brought in for the first time in the game, and many of us wondered if this wasn't too gimmicky and encroached on the relevance of the actual contest between bat and ball. We would know soon.

Sachin Tendulkar and I were batting together. He played a ball to point and I remember shouting 'No!' from the non-striker's end at the top of my voice, because I could see Jonty lurking at point. Alas, it was too late. Sachin had barely stepped a yard or so outside his crease for a single when Jonty swooped down on the ball and, in a flash, hit the stumps with a direct throw. Sachin, a fine runner between wickets, had barely started retracing his steps.

The entire sequence of dismissal couldn't have taken more than a couple of seconds. Jonty's speed and accuracy stunned everybody on the field. Even the umpires weren't sure. They went up to the third umpire for a referral. Sachin was found out of his crease. Thirty years later, I think I was lucky in not going for the single as I would have been run out by miles.

Thereafter, we were not only wary of Jonty, but, if truth be told, scared of him. Even if he was positioned a little deeper, we would avoid taking a run if the ball was hit in his direction. If the ball went past him, we settled for a single instead of attempting a risky second run. Mind you, we were playing a South African team that was renowned for its fielding prowess. But none of them had the same impact as Jonty. He put the fear of god in batsmen.

What put him a couple of notches higher than other great outfielders of my time – perhaps in the history of the game – was his uncanny anticipation. If you were playing off the back foot, he would be 3–4 yards towards the ball almost before you had even completed your stroke.

Having heels on wheels can give you speed, which is not to be scoffed at. But anticipation is something else. It is instinctive and intuitive. When allied to speed in running, it makes for deadly ability. This is what made Jonty into a global star.

WHITE LIGHTNING

Allan Donald

Allan Donald was lightning quick. Let me amend that a bit; he was *frighteningly* quick! South Africa – like Australia, England, West Indies (for a long while) and Pakistan – has a tradition of producing top-quality fast bowlers, and Allan is arguably the best they've ever had. To take 330 wickets in seventy-two Tests at an average of 22-odd puts him in the league of all-time greats.

Cricket historians will want to remind me about Peter Pollock from the past and Dale Steyn in recent years. There is no denying that these two are phenomenal fast bowlers, as borne out amply by their career statistics. But having faced Allan in his prime in 1992-93, I can't see any other South African bowler ahead of him.

As a side, we were always wary of Allan, who had come into the series with a mighty reputation forged in county cricket. Before the Tests began, a great deal of our discussions and planning centred on how to thwart him particularly. Our new coach then was Ajit Wadekar, no mean batsman against pace in his day, and he spent long hours trying to impress on us how to tackle this looming menace.

But theory is one thing. The proof of the pudding is in the playing. And, in this case, also in the suffering! Throughout that series, Allan haunted us like few fast bowlers had done. The pitches weren't particularly pacy or bouncy, yet in four tests he managed to get 20 wickets at an average below 20. He was that quick in the air!

Athletic and supremely fit, Allan covered a longish run up at full throttle. Legs like tree trunks gave him the traction to balance his delivery stride, honed over years of county cricket, perfectly. He put all his strength into his arm, shoulders and back for the delivery.

In that series in 1992-93, we didn't see him using too many variations. He didn't need them. He just ramped up speed and hit the spot slightly short of length – not easy to drive nor easy to play horizontal bat strokes – relentlessly, and kept us hopping and hoping. He was at his fastest and destructive best in the third Test at Port Elizabeth, picking up 12 wickets in the match on a slow pitch. But for a breathtaking, counter-attacking century by Kapil Dev, we would have finished under 100 instead of making 215, with Allan getting 7 wickets.

I first heard of Allan when playing for Glamorgan. Rodney Ontong from South Africa was a fellow pro at the county. One day, he mentioned there was a young kid from his country who wanted to bowl to us in the nets. I'd just returned from a fairly successful tour (for myself, as a batsman) of the West Indies in 1989, and was familiar with playing extreme pace. This possibly made me a trifle casual in the nets, and I found myself being tested severely by this young lad, who was bowling as fast Malcolm Marshall, Ian Bishop and Courtney Walsh.

Word about the young fast bowler spread rapidly on the circuit. Next season, Allan was snapped up by Warwickshire as an overseas recruit. The relationship lasted his entire career. I had asked Ontong later why he let Allan go to another county. I think he still regrets that.

Allan's transition from county to international cricket was smooth. I think he was yearning to be on the big stage, and prove himself against the best batsmen and teams. The break came at the right time for him. He was just about twenty-five when South Africa was reinstated as a Test nation in 1991 in international cricket. Further delay could have killed Allan's career and cost the game a great luminary.

For fast bowlers to succeed, their mental make-up should be right. They must be aggressive at all times, and this should be communicated effectively to batsmen; not through sledging or confrontation, but through speed, control and accuracy.

Allan was not guileful. He enjoyed bowling quick, and knew early on that he made the most impact with this. He was at batsmen all the time. A slightly square-on action made him very difficult to face, even more so when he went a little wide of the crease, slanting the ball back into the batsman, often chasing him.

Allan was the key man in South Africa beating India in that Test series, the first ever between the two countries. It was called the Friendship Series. His approach was anything but. As the next decade would show, he enjoyed scalping not just Indians, but players of all nationalities.

KING OF SPIN

Shane Warne

Shane Warne is the best spinner I've seen. Hang on, I'll extend the scope of that statement. He is perhaps the best spinner the game's ever seen. He may not have the record for the highest number of Test wickets, but what he could do with ball in his hand was magical and was the reason for many of Australia's victories in his era.

Some part of this praise comes from my own experience of playing against Warne. He made his debut in the Sydney Test against us in 1992, where both Sachin Tendulkar and I got centuries. Warne got only one wicket in the match, mine, after I had made 206, but this didn't stop him from giving me a dramatic 'send off' and pointing towards the pavilion disdainfully.

His bowling figures in that match were terribly unflattering – 1–150 – but you would have never guessed this from his demeanour on the field. He had a sharp tongue, as brash rookies – especially Aussie – usually do. But I realized during that innings itself that Warne had a sharp mind too.

He enjoyed mental jousts with batsmen from the beginning of his career, and his battle with Sachin – who was a few years younger than him, though a few years his senior in international cricket – was something I enjoyed watching from the other end. It would be dishonest of me to claim that I knew exactly how the careers of Sachin and Warne would play out, but I could sense their latent greatness even then. The young leg spinner hadn't had a productive debut, but there was no doubting his chutzpah.

At the post-match presentation ceremony, where I got the Man of the Match award for my double hundred, Warne walked past me, chest still puffed out, though it looked likely he might be dropped for the next Test. I found his positive attitude admirable. Holding him back briefly, I told Warne not to be disheartened, that he'd bowled really well and would be getting 6–7 wickets in an innings in the future for bowling far worse. Sure enough, he got 7–52 against West Indies soon after he had regained the favour of the selectors.

The turning point in Warne's career was getting Mike Gatting's wicket with the 'Ball of the Century' at Old Trafford in the first Test of the 1993 Ashes series. By then, Warne had proven himself in Sri Lanka and New Zealand as well as at home, and had become an integral member of the team.

Nothing stirs the imagination of fans and critics in Australia and England like the Ashes series and those who succeed in this contest. Gatting's wicket, which spurred Australia to a series win, also put Warne into the spotlight.

While this made him world famous overnight, it also put him under immense pressure. Apart from handling his new-found celebrity status, a task in itself, he would no longer be assessed by the earlier yardstick as a bowler; he'd changed the benchmark for himself. This can be very demanding on a young player. There are plenty of precocious young cricketers – batsmen and bowlers – who have fizzled out after a brilliant start when put to the test by opposing captains and players. Or because they couldn't cope with the pressure.

Warne, however, not only relished the attention, but saw it as motivation to get better and better. His career after 1993 takes on an upward trajectory that dipped but occasionally over the next fifteen years. Along with Glenn McGrath, he formed a pace–spin duo that took Australian cricket to great heights.

Skill itself can take a player only so far. It is the other attributes that make a player truly great. What stood out for me was Warne's temperament and readiness to compete in any situation. He was very tough in the mind, unwilling to ever give up. If the opposing side needed just a single to win a match and Warne was thrown the ball, he would make the batsman earn it. There were no gifts when he was bowling. Most of the half-volleys, full tosses or half-pitchers he bowled were to try and seduce the batsman into making errors.

Warne's ability to read a pitch, a match situation and set up batsmen was quite amazing. He was not only technically brilliant, but loved engaging in a battle of wills with batsmen, out-thinking them, and leading them to their doom. For this, control over line and length had to be impeccable. He was not a restrictive bowler; leg spinners rarely are, but Warne could veer towards the other extreme, of constantly attacking, not waiting to wear down batsmen. His strong wrist and shoulder would help give the ball a rip that few spinners have matched.

Most bowlers first experiment in the nets. Warne was unafraid to do this during a match if he felt it would work. This made his repertoire of deliveries inexhaustible. If he didn't have one planned for a particular pitch or situation, he would come up with one! Some of his deliveries would rate among the best in the history of the game. These were instrumental in changing the course of an innings (as happened most memorably in the 1996 World Cup semi-final against West Indies at Mohali), a Test and even a series.

Warne's track record in India, however, is not particularly impressive. During the 1998 series, in particular, I thought Indian batsmen, especially Sachin and Navjot Sidhu, thwarted him with excellent prior preparation, and then took the attack to him, not allowing him to settle. Even in 2001, he was still recovering from a shoulder injury and was below his best. Yet, he never gave it away.

I loved watching Warne in the middle, and I've enjoyed sharing the mic with him in the commentary box as much. He's got the gift of the gab and also a sharp mind. He can pick up nuances and trends in a match ahead of most, and like my all-time favourite Aussie, Ian Chappell, is always looking to take the game forward – as a player earlier, and now as an analyst. We share an excellent rapport and our conversations have ranged from poker to porn, with a lot of cricket in between!

Warne's status in the game is that of a titan. At a time when it looked like slow bowlers were becoming history, he, along with Muttiah Muralitharan and Anil Kumble, helped revive spin bowling. At his best, he was pure theatre, whether marking his run up or running in to bowl, or appealing for a dismissal. He didn't always succeed, but he managed to give batsmen sleepless nights.

A larger-than-life character who embellished and enriched cricket enormously.

INDIAN ATTACK'S LYNCHPIN

Anil Kumble

Anil Kumble was unquestionably the biggest match-winning bowler in Indian cricket. To take 600-plus Test wickets is an awesome feat by any reckoning and establishes him as an all-time great not just in India, but in the sport itself. He might have finished behind Muttiah Muralitharan and Shane Warne in tally of wickets, but Anil's influence on the game has been no less than the other two. Perhaps more, as he also captained India – a job that entails high pressure and demands.

Between them, these three great spinners revitalized spin bowling – which had seemed doomed to extinction once – and cricket has been richer since. When seen in the context of Indian cricket, bereft of pace support for most of his career, Anil's contribution becomes even more significant. His ability to run through sides on tracks even slightly helpful was mind-boggling.

Where other bowlers needed 35–40 overs for a 4-5 wicket haul, he would do this in 20–25 overs, effectively scuttling the opposing team's prospects of recovery.

Spotlighting Anil's prowess on Indian and subcontinental pitches does not in any way detract from his achievements. 'Home advantage' is a truism in cricket, but only if a player is able to make this count. Without ability, intelligence and ambition, such advantage is easily nullified. Of Anil's 619 wickets, 350 came in 63 home Tests. This is a fantastic strike rate and explains why he was the most feared Indian player when foreign teams toured the country. When you club these stats with his 269 wickets in 69 overseas Tests, his greatness is amplified.

Anil's prowess on home (and subcontinental pitches) is best highlighted by his 10-wicket haul in a single innings against Pakistan at Delhi in 1998-99. I was doing commentary for a large chunk of time as Anil joined Jim Laker to become the second bowler in cricket history to take all 10 wickets in an innings. What came through was not just his exemplary control, but also aggressive intent. Once he sensed that the Pakistan batsmen were on tenterhooks against him, he went in for the kill.

Anil's gentlemanly conduct – on and off the field – did not mean he was a namby-pamby cricketer. He was fiercely competitive and aggressive, unsparing of even his teammates if they showed signs of slacking.

I was his first room partner when we went to Sharjah in 1990. Tall and well-built, but shy, Anil largely kept to himself and spoke only when spoken to. With his oversized spectacles and quiet demeanour, he looked more like a professor than an international sportsman. These initial perceptions changed swiftly as he began to demonstrate his skills on the field.

STARGAZING   177

After a hesitant start to his Test career in England in 1990,
Anil rose to pre-eminence in the next few years, both as a bowler
and an influential voice in the dressing room. It helped that India
played a lot of matches at home, and on tracks that assisted spin,
in which our then coach Ajit Wadekar had a big role. Success
boosted Anil's confidence, and fuelled his ambition. But he didn't
rest on laurels; instead, he constantly endeavoured to learn more
of his craft and speedily became the lynchpin of India's bowling
attack in the early 1990s itself.

His great strengths as a bowler were accuracy, control and
the bounce he derived because of his height. Not a great spinner
of the ball, the variations and improvisations he employed were
subtle and nuanced, stemming from pinpoint precision in line
and length.

Strong shoulders and a high arm, side-on action are the basics
of technique that all young bowlers – fast or slow – are taught
when growing up. This is the fulcrum for balance in bowling.
But often, not enough importance is given to the other shoulder
and its positioning in the delivery stride. Anil, however, made
excellent use of his left shoulder for balance, which in turn
gave him immaculate control and accuracy. His tenacity was
exemplified best in the West Indies in 2002, when he bowled 14
overs with a broken jaw. I can hardly remember him leaving the
field for any ailment or hurt. Not for him fatigue or boredom,
which some players try to camouflage as injury.

As a bowler, he was steadfast and purposeful, unyielding in
concentration and determination. As a captain, he was tactically
sound, and led with authority and expertise. He got the captaincy
late in his career (not trusting a bowler with this job is my
eternal bugbear against administrators and selectors), but left an

indelible impact in the brief while he was in charge. I thought his handling of Monkeygate in 2008 was commendable for its maturity and firmness. It was too sophisticated for the cribbing Aussies, but earned the respect of one and all everywhere else.

FROM

THE

BOX

MASTER AND COMMANDER

Sourav Ganguly

Sourav Ganguly ranks – quite rightly – among the most influential cricket players, not just in India, but in the sport itself. He was made captain of the Indian team at a very difficult time after the unsavoury match-fixing scam broke in 2000. Indian cricket was in a shambles. Fans were understandably angry and dejected. Considering the number of names that were tossed around in the inquiries and the court cases that followed in different countries, the reputation of the game was massively sullied.

Sourav was still a youngster, having made his debut only four years earlier. To a lot of people on the outside, the BCCI's decision to make him captain didn't seem too clever. Some fellow cricketers too felt this way. I remember there was much

cluck-clucking among former players when he was chosen to
lead the side.

What were the apprehensions? Sourav had had very little
experience of captaincy at that point in time. Moreover, he
was emerging as a major batsman and being handed over the
captaincy in such a deep crisis would, it was feared, affect his
batting. Captaining the Indian team is always onerous, and these
were extraordinary circumstances.

Among the seniors in the team, Sachin Tendulkar had just
resigned the captaincy. Anil Kumble and Javagal Srinath had
both been around for a decade, but selectors everywhere in the
world are reluctant to make frontline bowlers captain. Rahul
Dravid was the only other option. It was a toss-up between the
two. Sourav got the nod, and it proved to be a turning point in
Indian cricket.

For someone so young and inexperienced, Sourav handled
the responsibility with remarkable aplomb. Some players come
into their own when circumstances are most difficult. Sourav
showed his mettle during his captaincy, leading the team with
confidence, imagination and flair. The first Test series he
captained was against Australia in 2001. The Aussies were on
the rampage in those days, having won sixteen Tests on the trot,
before being stopped by Sourav's team. After losing the Mumbai
Test, India were on the ropes before the sensational turnaround
in Kolkata. The team's victory in Chennai not only clinched the
rubber, but also breathed new life into Indian cricket.

I must rewind a bit and talk about my earliest impression
of Sourav. We were together on the tour of Australia in
1991-92. I was a decade old in international cricket by then; he
was a promising youngster whom many people had spoken

highly of. Unfortunately, Sourav didn't get to play in any of the five Tests on that tour. Shy and reserved, he kept largely to himself, or spent time with Sachin with whom he had played at the junior level. He was of slender build, but packed a lot of punch in his strokes when he played in the nets. He always looked eager to make an impact, but with so many established batsmen around, he failed to impress the tour selection committee, even though we were struggling as a unit.

Apart from his batting, Sourav was also a handy medium-pacer, able to swing and cut the ball, which caught my interest. I was representing the Tatas in club cricket back home, and we were looking for an all-rounder of his kind. I spoke about Sourav to the Tata cricket team management, and he was soon recruited by the club.

For all the potential he showed so early, Sourav disappeared from the national scene for a few years. But it hadn't done his form any harm, as he showed when he resurfaced on the radar of the national selectors. His skills had been honed further, and he was also more mature, ready to make a mark at the highest level.

With centuries in his first two Tests against England in 1996, he was off to a galloping start in international cricket, making up for lost time with style and determination. He fit into the Indian team smoothly, becoming a key constituent in the formidable batting line-up that would emerge with Dravid, V.V.S. Laxman and, later, Virender Sehwag joining Sachin.

One hardly need spend too many words on Sourav's batting. He was an elegant batsman, with offside strokes that were nothing short of majestic. His arms flowed freely when he was playing off the front foot, and a strong bottom hand would come in for those off the back foot. His penchant for lofted shots in front of the wicket served him – and the team – excellently in ODIs. He could clear the infield with ease, and batting at the top, made the most of field restrictions. Along with Sachin, Sourav formed one of the great opening partnerships in limited-overs cricket.

His lasting impact, of course, is as captain. He was a very good reader of the game, and would get under the skin of opponents, which served him and the team well, especially when playing at home. What stood out most was the faith and the conviction he showed in the youngsters in the team. A whole bunch of players who served India with distinction – Viru, Yuvraj Singh, Harbhajan Singh, Zaheer Khan – started out and grew into match-winning performers under his leadership. Captaincy is not just about tactics but also trusting in talent.

My relationship with Sourav has often come under the spotlight. Our so-called 'differences' have been chaat and bhelpuri for the media, which went to town on them, especially because of the dynamics in selecting the chief coach in 2016 and 2017. In fact, it was nothing more than two people seeing the same situation differently.

SPIN WIZARD

Muttiah Muralitharan

Could Muttiah Muralitharan spin the ball even on glass? I don't remember when, but I did ask him this as a rhetorical question once. He didn't answer, but his quizzical look seemed to say, 'Do you doubt this?'

Having watched Muralitharan bowl in several series and tournaments, in both Tests and limited-overs cricket, from the commentary box, I can say, without hesitation, that he was a genius. True, he bowled with a bent elbow, and was subjected to severe scrutiny for his action, especially in the early part of his career, but medical tests showed that the flex was natural, which is good enough for me. This was a handicap and Muralitharan deserves credit, not brickbats, for turning it into an advantage.

For a while, in the mid-1990s, when he was called out for chucking in Australia, I thought his career might take a nosedive.

But Muralitharan found a staunch supporter and mentor in Arjuna Ranatunga, and survived that trauma to become a champion bowler. He owes his former captain around 600 of his 800 Test wickets!

His career stats, which I checked recently, are astonishing. The strike rate is 55, which is fantastic for a slow bowler. He's taken 5 wickets in an innings sixty-seven times and 10 wickets in a match on twenty-two occasions, which is incredible! Against England at the Oval in 1998, he picked up his career-best Test wicket haul of 16 wickets, 9 of which were in the second innings (one batsman was run out). Barring Jim Laker, who got 19 wickets against Australia at Old Trafford in 1956, no other spinner has got so many wickets in a match in England.

Muralitharan's biggest strength was his ability to get turn on any surface. Though an off-spinner, he could actually spin the ball both ways. With him, the doosra was not the delivery which went through with the arm, holding its line, but turned like a genuine leg break.

Over the years, subsequent bowlers have tried to acquire this skill, and, among current spinners, Ravichandran Ashwin is a master at it. Even so, Muralitharan was unique. He could use his wrist to bowl off-spin and fingers to bowl leg spin! The flex in his arm enabled him to turn the ball on any pitch and to a substantial degree. Normally, wrist spinners get more turn and bounce, but Murali could surpass even them by using just his fingers.

Like all great bowlers of pace or spin, Murali's mastery over line, length and turn was impeccable. The last attribute is particularly important, especially on pitches that afford help to slow bowlers. Too much turn is actually counterproductive as it can take leg before wicket decisions out of the equation.

But while accuracy and control are at the core of good spin bowling, deception is at the heart of great spin bowling. This is what made Murali, like the other genius Shane Warne, the nemesis of batsmen. He could make the best batsmen double guess their decisions and entice them into error as if this was routine work. Of course, it wasn't. It's just that Murali was a wizard.

NO ESCAPE FOR BATSMEN

Glenn McGrath

 Glenn McGrath was without doubt one of the most formidable fast bowlers of his time. He was not of express pace, which meant that he had to develop other weapons to pick up wickets. That he finished with 563 Test sticks at an average of 21.6 shows just how good he was.

McGrath's greatest strength was his control over line and length. This might seem clichéd, but when one considers that he seldom faltered in these attributes, whether playing in Australia, England, India, South Africa or wherever else, it becomes remarkable.

Over 90 per cent of bowlers take time to adjust to pitches and conditions in different countries. The rest who manage to do this swiftly are from the top drawer. McGrath not only adjusted and adapted almost immediately, but was also a serious wicket-taker in every cricket-playing country, which puts him in the top 5 per cent in the history of the game.

His consistency was amazing. I've been behind the microphone for almost all his matches against India – home and overseas – as well as ICC tournaments, and marvelled at his superb technique and fierce commitment to excellence. Over after over, match after match, series after series, he would land on the right spot eight times out of ten. This shows how quickly he could assess pitches, for no two 22-yard strips are identical even in the same country, let alone the world. There wasn't a single surface where you could take him lightly. Even on a feather bed, he'd find the right length and line to hold batsmen on a leash. If there was any juice in the track, batsmen were in woe.

I've talked about control and consistency as his best virtues, but McGrath also had ample skills. In fact, he was among those fast bowlers who could swing the ball in the air as well as seam it off the pitch with equal facility, not unlike the great Richard Hadlee. This combination of excellent swing and seam bowling made him dangerous even though he lacked high pace. Moreover, where fast bowlers tend to slacken their effort on slow pitches in frustration, McGrath would revel in such conditions.

On sluggish tracks and in conditions unfavourable to fast bowlers, he would introduce variations of pace and length with nagging accuracy, and dismiss even well-set batsmen in conditions not favouring fast bowlers with remarkable frequency. There would be no let-up in his aggression.

Another trait McGrath shared with Hadlee was utter professionalism. Both were feisty and combustible. But while they could lose their temper every now and then, they never let this affect their control. Many bowlers – fast and slow – lose their cool if hit by batsmen for too many runs, or if a fielder drops a catch, or if there is a lot of play and miss, with luck not going their way. Their control slips and, with mounting anger, so does the prospect of claiming wickets.

McGrath, like Hadlee, would recover swiftly from a bout of ill luck, becoming even more resolute to get the better of the batsman. The pace would go up a notch, control over length would become sharper, and the batsman would be probed evermore. This kept opponents from getting under his skin, especially after he became a major player and realized that getting into scraps with batsmen was unnecessary. And if a scrap was inevitable, he'd recover his wits quickly and bowl even better.

McGrath was a very intense competitor. He never yielded an inch, not even when the match was petering out towards a draw. He loved big matches. They would prime him up to play at his best. The more reputed the batsman in front of him, the more motivated he would be and the harder he would strive. His contests against Sachin Tendulkar and Brian Lara, the two best batsmen at that point, are the stuff of legend.

In the 1999 World Cup, India had to beat Australia to stay alive in the tournament, but McGrath got his main prey – Sachin – early, and the team collapsed. In the 2003 World Cup, after Australia had posted a mammoth total, India's hopes had rested squarely on an in-form Sachin getting a big score. McGrath felled the maestro in the very first over, snuffing out India's chances right at the beginning.

Australia has a long and rich tradition of producing great fast bowlers, Ray Lindwall and Dennis Lillee among them. Glenn McGrath has certainly earned the right to be placed on the same pedestal as these two.

STALLONE MEETS SCHWARZENEGGER

Matthew Hayden

Matthew Hayden is not the kind of man you want to mess with on a cricket field – or even in arm-wrestling. I am not slight of build, mind you, but meeting this imposing specimen for the first time, even I felt puny.

Tall, barrel-chested, with a slim waist, big hands and arms, and legs like tree trunks, he looked a cross between Stallone and Schwarzenegger, oozing power from every inch of his massive frame. I could well imagine why bowlers dreaded him in the middle.

I started paying serious attention to Hayden during Australia's tour of India in 2001. Some Aussie cricketers I was in touch with told me to watch out for the big left-hander. 'Powerful striker,' said one. 'The big threat to your side,' another cautioned. All of which seemed a trifle exaggerated at the time.

Steve Waugh's team, apart from the captain himself, boasted of his brother Mark Waugh, Michael Slater, Justin Langer and upcoming youngster Ricky Ponting – a clutch of fantastic batsmen. What could be so special about Hayden? Moreover, several promising overseas batsmen had been bested on slow turners.

By the end of the series, though, Hayden had scored the most runs from either side. More than even the brilliant V.V.S. Laxman. What impressed was that the Aussie left-hander not only played slow bowling well, but how brilliantly he read and adjusted to the pitches to take the attack to the spinners.

With his long reach, he used the sweep and slog-sweep brilliantly to unsettle bowlers. Not since Graham Gooch had swept us out of the 1987 World Cup semi-final had an overseas batsman played this shot so effectively. But while Gooch had done this in one match, Hayden did it in all three Tests, clinching the series for his team almost single-handedly.

Only batsmen of very high calibre bat like this on subcontinental pitches. For someone who grew up at the pacy Gabba to work out a way to master spin on Indian pitches showed deep intent backed by a lot of hard work in the nets and mental preparation. My view about Hayden was hastily revised.

Over the next few years, he went a few notches higher in my esteem, particularly in 2002, when I was in South Africa on a commentary assignment. Australia v South Africa does not have the romance of the Ashes, nor the new-found competitive richness of Australia v India, but it is a bitterly fought contest nonetheless.

Having high-quality fast bowlers in both teams means there is a lot of aggro and bouncers involved. This series was played under a lot of tension too. Hayden showed up marvellously in the rubber, taming an attack that had Allan Donald, Makhaya Ntini, Jacques Kallis and André Nel. He batted with supreme authority, and breathtaking strokes. Adam Gilchrist and Ponting made a lot of runs too, but they benefited from Hayden's dominant batting at the top. In the two years that I had been following his career regularly, he had shown adaptability, skill and toughness to succeed in all conditions.

Together with Virender Sehwag, Hayden was the most destructive and intimidating opening batsman in the first decade of this century. Both batsmen flayed bowling attacks all over the world, that too in brutal fashion, leaving bowlers and opposing captains in despair. While it may have appeared from the outside that they were slam-bang hitters, both worked out the percentages of the shots they played very shrewdly. Theirs were calculated assaults, not mindless slogging; the point of departure being that Viru had more bravado while Hayden used more muscle. What separates sloggers from genuine attacking batsmen is the latter's consistency in scoring and performance in big innings. Both these batsmen come through this litmus test superbly. In fact, it's uncanny how similar their Test batting stats are in terms of matches and innings played, runs scored and career averages. Both had fairly long careers, made runs everywhere, with plentiful centuries each. For good measure, both also have a triple ton (Viru has two) to their credit. Such run-scoring can't be a fluke; rather, it is a sign of greatness. But more than the stats, it was the fear they put into their rivals, which gave their respective teams big advantage.

First with Slater and then Langer, Hayden formed hugely productive opening partnerships which helped win Tests at home and overseas. Coming in at the top of the order, he and Gilchrist caused mayhem for years in white-ball cricket, apart from helping win important titles.

Hayden was a pivotal figure in the great Australian team between 1995 and 2008. A lot of attention – and for good reason – has been heaped on Steve and Mark Waugh, Ponting, Shane Warne, Glenn McGrath and Gilchrist, but not enough on Hayden, without whom the Aussies may not have been as successful in that period.

We hit it off at our first meeting and our friendship has grown over the years. Whenever the 'Big Fella' is in town, which has been fairly often since he retired, we find time to catch up over a drink and a long cigar.

Hayden's call-it-as-I-see-it commentary has won him millions of new fans, and his 'masterchef' skills have endeared him to a completely different world of admirers here, making India, as he puts it, his second home.

FIGHT TO WIN

Ricky Ponting

 Ricky Ponting's aggressive approach, strong instinct to counter-attack, and unbending desire to dominate the bowling made him a dangerous adversary, but a marvellous sight to watch from the stands or commentary box.

From the time I first saw him in 1996, when he came to India, Ponting impressed me with his competitive instincts. He looked eager to be in the thick of the action, and I remember him – a rookie – trying to get the ear of captain Mark Taylor, and have his say in the proceedings. It wasn't a very happy tour for Ponting as a batsman, though, and made worse by the controversy surrounding him: breaking curfew and heading to the bar, and other such misdemeanours which are frowned upon by all team managements.

Some of cricket's legendary players have been romanticized for their exotic parallel lifestyles. And while such indulgences may not have raised any eyebrows in the past, they are certainly not kosher in the modern, professional game. With the passage of time, the demands from players evolve. The emphasis on fitness and 100 per cent focus is necessary to get players to give their best, without which it becomes difficult to justify the financial rewards that come their way.

However, I've always believed that disapproval of how young cricketers behave must not extend to summary rejection. The process of growing up from teenage into adulthood shows up many vulnerabilities. These must be tackled with understanding and empathy, not just a show of power.

Fortunately, Ponting was warned, but not discarded for his mistakes. Cricket Australia's sensitive handling and mentoring ensured that one of their most promising youngsters went on to become an all-time great, instead of finishing as a what-might-have-been story of regret.

In the years that followed, Ponting developed into a truly formidable cricketer, and perhaps the best all-round fielder of his time. In the deep, his dazzling speed helped him cover ground swiftly to save runs; he took blinders in the slips, and hit bullseye from covers or mid-on more regularly than other player I'd seen except Viv Richards.

His fielding prowess – a combination of speed, reflexes and athleticism, to a large degree – explained why he was such a good batsman too, especially against fast bowlers where the reaction time is usually a nanosecond. With the bat, he was nimble on his feet, equally at ease off front foot and back, revelled in the hook, cut and pull strokes (as most Aussie batsmen do), and was among the swiftest runners between the wickets. Then there was the tempo at which he scored, which invariably put his team into a strong, if not winning, position.

He was pugnacious and loved a scrap, always waiting to hand out two punches in return for every one he received. If I have to draw a parallel with boxing, among the players I've seen, Viv Richards was the heavyweight champion, and Ponting would come in at light-heavy.

Against India, he had his problems early on when Harbhajan troubled him incessantly with bite and turn on home tracks. Over time, though, he learnt to cope with Indian pitches and racked up some very fine knocks to his credit, especially a Test century in the 2008-09 series, and two years later, in the quarter-final of the World Cup against India.

Overseas, of course, he was India's nemesis. His century at the Wanderers, in the 2003 World Cup final against India remains unforgettable. Coming in one drop, he pulverized the bowling with breathtaking strokes. By the time he was dismissed, the match was over for all practical purposes. During 2003-04, he was in devastating form and made more runs than any other batsman from either side. But then, whenever we played in Australia, he was destructive.

As captain too, Ponting's record is highly impressive. He was not as astute as Mark Taylor or as cussedly determined as Allan Border. However, the intent to win was predominant, which meant that the opponents were always under pressure. Like good leaders, he led from the front.

Statistics place Ponting among the best batsmen from Australia. Behind Don Bradman, of course, but to be clubbed alongside Greg Chappell, Neil Harvey, Allan Border and, from the current lot, Steve Smith – who are some of the greatest in the game – is a rare, but well-deserved honour.

HEAVYWEIGHT HITTER

Jacques Kallis

I was doing commentary in South Africa in Jacques Kallis's last Test when I realized that his batting and catching record more or less matched Rahul Dravid's, and the bowling stats were similar to Zaheer Khan's! Considering that Dravid and Zak are among the finest players in the game in the past twenty to twenty-five years, Kallis's cricketing credentials become even more stellar.

For good measure, Kallis scored a century in his final Test which helped South Africa beat India and clinch the series. He was thirty-eight and looked good for a couple of years more at least. Neither his reflexes, speed between wickets or pace in the bowling seem to have suffered.

But the best players are loath to plod on and become lacklustre performers. The signal to quit can come from the body or the mind. I suppose he was jaded from having played non-stop for eighteen years.

Kallis had by then played 166 Tests and 328 ODIs. The statistical aspect of his career is dazzling. In red-ball international cricket, he had 13,289 runs and claimed 292 wickets, in the 50-over format he had 11,579 runs and 273 wickets. The best attributes of a cricketer are defined by success in the five-day format. In Tests, Kallis had averaged 55.37, higher than other batting superstars of his era barring Kumar Sangakkara, but including Sachin Tendulkar, Brian Lara, Ricky Ponting and Dravid.

His 292 Test wickets came at an average of 32.65. This may not seem as imposing as his batting record, but when you juxtapose the two functions, the bowling figures are no less impressive. And there are 200 catches too. Extraordinary!

You would not want to compare anyone with Gary Sobers, but if there is one player who provokes such comparison, it is Kallis. The numbers stack up in his favour more than for any other all-rounder. Apart from Sobers, Kallis is perhaps the only player who could walk into any side on batting or bowling ability alone on consistency of performance over a long period of time. Imran Khan, Ian Botham and Kapil Dev were equally good in either department for some number of years, but not over almost two decades.

I would imagine a small pool of cricketers compels development of all-round skills, which is why South Africa boasts such a rich legacy of quality all-rounders, more than any other country in the past fifty or sixty years. Eddie Barlow, Mike Procter, Clive Rice – against whom I played a lot in county cricket – Brian McMillan, Shaun Pollock, Lance Klusener, were all world-class players.

Kallis, like Pollock and Klusener, had a full playing life unlike Procter, Rice and McMillan who lost several years (Procter and Rice almost their entire careers) because of the apartheid-linked ban imposed on South Africa. But even so, Kallis's wondrous exploits leave no doubt where he stands, irrespective of the era.

Powerfully built, with an Arnold Schwarzenegger-like torso and legs as sturdy as oak trees, Kallis became the pivotal figure in the South African team from the time of his debut till he retired because of his multi-tasking prowess. He was tireless, capable of batting long hours with great concentration, or bowling long spells without flagging.

Unlike most all-rounders who tend to be flamboyant in one or both functions, Kallis was classically orthodox and a hard-nosed, hard-working, high-quality, high-achieving cricketer. His game was structured on solid technique, which lent easily to finesse. This made him attractive to watch and hard to get the better of.

In a team that had Graeme Smith, Hashim Amla and A.B. de Villiers, his was still the hardest wicket to get. With a wide repertoire of strokes at his command – those on the off-side being his hallmark – he could tame the best bowling attack, wearing it down with immaculate defence or controlled aggression.

As a bowler he didn't get the accolades he deserved. Playing alongside Allan Donald, Pollock, Makhaya Ntini and Dale Steyn, all superb pacemen, cast him in a supporting role. But on his day, Kallis could be their equal in pace and skill.

Many Indian batsmen of his time told me he was the most difficult to face because of the shoulder and back strength he put into his bowling, getting awkward bounce even on lifeless pitches.

For around six or seven years, the South Africans were the best performing side overseas. Kallis's versatility and ability to adapt to different conditions quickly was a big reason for this. What surprises me, though, is that they failed to win any major ICC title despite having a player of Kallis's supreme ability in their ranks.

Very unassuming and low key despite his magnificent achievements, Kallis is a real heavyweight in the annals of the game.

MIGHTY WALL

Rahul Dravid

Like Sunil Gavaskar before him, Rahul Dravid was the bulwark of the Indian team in his era. I watched him play from the time he made his debut in 1996 till he walked off the field for the last time in 2012, and he belonged to a category of batsmen all too rare in the sport – even more so now with the proliferation of T20.

Dravid was the fulcrum of India's batting. With his resolve and capacity to bat for long periods unflinchingly against the best attacks and in the most daunting circumstances, he not only scored thousands of runs himself, but allowed other batsmen in the side to bat more freely. To be honest, some of the accolades these batsmen received should have actually accrued to him!

His strength of character came through not just in the tough situations he overcame, but also how he slipped into a supporting role without ever trying to upstage his partner. The true value of his batting is revealed when you go through the stats for the series he played in: he was usually the leading or second-highest run-scorer, without any show of flamboyance.

Dravid had a watertight technique and a temperament that could not be distracted from the task on hand. His powers of concentration were astonishing. He could bat an entire day – as he and V.V.S. Laxman did so memorably in Kolkata in 2001 – without wavering in attention, simply gritting his teeth and sticking to the task. That he has 200 catches to his credit, a majority of them while fielding in the slips, further highlights the focus he brought to his game.

Apart from being technically superb, Dravid was gutsy, intelligent and diligent. He worked very hard on his game to become among the most formidable batsman of his generation. He was not called the 'Wall' for nothing. Once he settled down in the crease, he was a most difficult batsman to remove. Bowlers and rival captains would be reduced to hand-wringing frustration as he shut out everything else from his mind, made occupation of the crease and scoring runs his sole purpose. Barring his last series in Australia in 2011-12 where every Indian batsman struggled, Dravid's consistency in a sixteen-year career is remarkable. He batted as if his life depended on it. Every batsman strives to do this, but not all have this fierce determination.

He wasn't a grungy, unattractive stonewaller. He had an attractive cover drive, played the square cut beautifully and had an amazing pull shot. These strokes are usually the staple of attacking batsmen. Dravid had made defence his forte for a purpose. It's often overlooked that he scored almost 11,000 ODI runs too!

Most major batsmen develop their skills swiftly through watching, learning and playing, reach their peak by the time they hit thirty, then plateau at a level of excellence which becomes their hallmark. Dravid was among the few I saw who kept evolving with each passing match, series and year. In 2011, at thirty-eight, he scored three centuries in four Tests in England, countering the late, probing swing of James Anderson, Stuart Broad and Tim Bresnan with jaw-dropping technical finesse. He had made three centuries in four Tests in England earlier too, in 2002. The one at Headingley was particularly memorable for how he blunted England's pace attack in conditions tailor-made for them and notched up 600-plus runs. Still, I believe Dravid in 2011 was exceptional; not just because he was in the evening of his career, but also because Indian batting, unlike in 2002, was struggling badly.

From 2002 till he retired a decade later, Dravid was at his peak. The series in Australia in 2003-04, when he scored over 600 runs again, announced him as a world-class batsman. While conditions for batsmen can often be more challenging in England, where technique is concerned, playing the Aussies is tougher because of their no-quarter-given approach, especially when facing them in their own backyard. The pitches are harder, with extra pace and bounce, and the close-in fielders are always in the 'ears' of the batsmen with the choicest of words and phrases to distract and demoralize. But Dravid remained unfazed in the face of the Aussie attack. The bounce and pace didn't unsettle him, nor did the sledging.

In fact, in time, his indifference to these tactics came to be so well known that not just the Aussies, but all opponents recognized the futility of trying to needle him. The more his opponents tried to provoke him, the stronger he became mentally, getting even more focused and tighter in his batting. He's played poor shots, sure. All batsmen do over the course of their careers, even the best in the world. Yet, I can't remember an occasion when Dravid threw his wicket away because he got cheesed off with the banter around him.

Although India drew the Test series against England (2002) and Australia (2003-04), Dravid played a stellar role in both. While Sachin Tendulkar was dominating the world stage, Dravid was just as consistent, weathering many storms.

I found him very impressive as a captain as well, an aspect of his cricket career which hasn't got enough attention. He led India to Test series' wins in the West Indies and England after decades, and was instrumental in India beating Pakistan on their home ground for the first time ever, scoring two centuries and guiding the team with sensible attacking captaincy.

Off the field, Dravid is relaxed and easy-going, not as intense as he used to be in his playing days. As coach, I've been in touch with him regularly, inquiring about young players he's mentored in the Under-19 or Under-25 age groups. He's always been up to date and forthright in his assessments. A great batsman and true role model, Dravid is earnest, dedicated, and very good with youngsters because he has an open mind and puts in serious effort to understand them. In his new avatar as director of cricket operations at the National Cricket Academy, he should do a fabulous job. I hope at some stage he will take up the reins as India coach too.

EPIC CHASER

V.V.S. Laxman

 V.V.S. Laxman does not have the batting average of a Sachin Tendulkar or a Rahul Dravid, but his contribution to Indian cricket is memorable for the number of important match-winning innings he's played. His back-to-the-wall 281 against Australia at Kolkata in 2001 was one such epic innings that redefined Indian cricket.

When I started played county cricket for Glamorgan in 1987, people were still discussing Ian Botham's incredible 149 in the 1981 Headingley Test that helped England win against all odds after being asked to follow on. VVS's performance in 2001 was no less impactful.

Australia had come to Kolkata on the back of sixteen consecutive wins. India was still reeling from a massive defeat at Mumbai in the first Test. More despairingly, the shadow of the match-fixing scandal involving Hansie Cronje and a clutch of home players loomed over the country. The odds were stacked heavily in favour of Australia.

How this hopeless situation was transformed into a winning one makes for a remarkable story. It hinges on one of the great partnerships in the history of cricket – 376 between VVS and Rahul Dravid – and one whole day when Australia failed to dislodge either. I was privileged to be doing commentary for that match, which allowed me to see VVS's mastery first-hand.

For all practical purposes, the Test and the series was lost after India were bundled out cheaply and asked to follow on by Steve Waugh. Then came the VVS–Dravid partnership that turned the match on its head. Both batsmen had a point to prove. VVS, with a half-century in the first innings when the other batsmen had failed, was promoted to number three in the second innings. He grabbed this opportunity to leave his stamp with the innings of a lifetime. Dravid, pushed down the order from number three to number six, would have been determined to regain his original position.

The way these two, especially VVS, thwarted and then tamed the Aussie bowling attack is the stuff of legend. Glenn McGrath was a threat on any surface, but by the fourth day, as the wicket started showing wear and tear, the bigger danger came from Shane Warne. How VVS dismantled Warne was an object lesson in attacking batsmanship against a top-class spinner on a pitch that had turn. He read Warne from his hand, went back and cut him against the spin in vacant spots on the offside, or stepped down the track for drives on either side of the wicket. No matter what Warne threw at him, VVS refused to allow him to settle down. The amazing knock of 281 elevated him into the big league, and made India's batting history considerably richer.

A wristy and stylish player like his predecessor from Hyderabad, Mohammad Azharuddin, VVS was an aesthete's delight. Unlike Azhar, who was slender and sprightly with wrists that seemed to have flubber in them, VVS was more heavily built, the wrists less tensile, and played more in the V, at least to start with. While Azhar's stroke play could be exotic, VVS was more in control, especially in defence. His excellent improvisation skills would come into play the longer he batted. And he had steel in his spine. Adverse conditions and situations brought out the best in him. While comparisons with Azhar are not unjustified in batting similarities, I think VVS was more like Gundappa Viswanath from the 1970s. He rose a notch higher under pressure, delivering when the team needed it most.

Few have batted better than VVS on the hard, bouncy tracks in Australia or on the slow turners in India, which shows his versatility and capacity to adjust. Against pace and spin, he was one of the finest timers of the ball in his day. He hardly ever slogged the ball into the air; he didn't need to because he found gaps in the field so easily. Batting in the company of tailenders brought out his best improvisations. He was an astute reader of what the opposition would try to do and adapted his game accordingly. In farming the strike, I'd say VVS was just a shade behind Miandad, the best I've seen, and on par with Steve Waugh.

He wasn't the swiftest runner between the wickets and in the field, but one must remember he played with dodgy knees for most of his career. Running ability never remains the same after your knees have been operated on. Ask me; it ended my career early. Still, VVS worked very hard to maintain the standards required, and, in the process, became an excellent slip fielder.

I have a lot of admiration for VVS. He's soft-spoken, but not malleable. As he did in the middle, he can stand his ground on any issue with conviction, but without rancour. A likeable man who played for the country with pride and excellence, leaving an everlasting impact.

STYLE AND SUBSTANCE

Mahela Jayawardene

 Mahela Jayawardene, like V.V.S. Laxman, was a tremendous timer of the cricket ball and among the most attractive batsmen to watch.

Timing the ball can be difficult on the slow turners found in the subcontinent. For guys like VVS and Mahela, however, this is not a problem. They play late, often choosing the stroke at the last second, leaving the bowler and fielding side bewildered. What would be a high-risk shot for most batsmen becomes a productive one for these touch artists.

Mahela had a terrific repertoire of strokes to choose from, along with a fine defence. Fluent drives on either side of the pitch, delectable glances and late cuts, a fierce cut shot, hooks and pulls played with superb control. When not playing attacking strokes, he would find a vacant nook or corner in the field with a nudge or a push, bringing tensile wrists into play. His footwork was sure, and the strokes – whether defensive or attacking – played with style and assurance. Small-statured, he was quick on his feet, decisive in playing off front or back foot, or stepping out to the pitch of the ball with dainty steps against slow bowlers.

Whatever the surface, and however briefly he batted, Mahela's innings were always graceful, a work of art. Sometimes, batsmen lose rhythm and try as they might, can't get the ball off the square. I have hardly ever seen Mahela struggle. He may have got out cheaply playing a poor shot but it rarely looked ugly.

Sri Lanka have always produced outstanding batsmen. When we toured there in 1985, Duleep Mendis and Roy Dias took our bowling to task. Succeeding Mendis and Dias were Arjuna Ranatunga and Aravinda De Silva. Sanath Jayasuriya and Tillakaratne Dilshan held the batting together after Ranatunga and Aravinda retired. But, without doubt, the best batting pair from the island country has been Mahela and Kumar Sangakkara. Between them, they topped 24,000 Test runs! Once they got in, the right–left combo made life despairingly difficult for opponents.

Mahela made runs by the tons in his own country, but not in equal measure overseas. This is sometimes held as an argument against his virtuosity. Which is hogwash. Coaches and captains who played Sri Lanka at the time will tell you they spent as much time planning out Mahela's wicket as Sangakkara's. A tremendous all-wicket player, Mahela was great to watch when in full flow. All shots by the book, and timed perfectly. I thought his 103 not out in the 2011 World Cup final was a classic. He took his time to settle in after a couple of wickets had fallen early and then, in a huge pressure game, just upped the ante with some breathtaking stroke play, especially towards the end.

In hindsight, the victory looks simpler than it was, when in fact Mahela's knock put India under the pump. M.S. Dhoni and Co. had to play some outstanding cricket to win.

As captain too, Mahela did extremely well by his team. He has a good mind for the game, and was constantly plotting and planning shrewdly, without being demonstrative, which could lull opponents into errors. His acuity and knowledge have also helped him make a big impact in the IPL as coach for the Mumbai Indians team.

Of fine cricketing etiquette and accomplishments, Mahela was an embellishment to the sport.

NEVER BACK DOWN

Harbhajan Singh

Harbhajan Singh was a crucial part of the Indian bowling attack during the decade he played cricket for India. In Bhajji, Anil Kumble found a fantastic ally, and Bhajji a mentor in Kumble. The two struck up a partnership that would win many matches for the country.

Bhajji was a feisty cricketer. I observed almost his entire career from the commentary box, met with him frequently and never found him bored, fatigued or cold to a challenge. From the moment he made his debut, he was hungry for success; even criticism about his action did not faze him. Players with lesser determination would have become morose and dejected, for his career was on the line, but Bhajji became more resolute. He sorted out the problem swiftly, and became a better and

more dangerous bowler, as the Aussies learnt in the dramatic
2001 series.

Steve Waugh's team was unarguably the best in the world
then and on a winning streak. India were without Kumble, their
champion bowler, especially on home pitches. Much has been
spoken and written about how V.V.S. Laxman and Rahul Dravid
turned the series around at Kolkata with their magnificent
partnership, but Bhajji's role in India winning the series was
no less significant. He took a whopping 32 wickets in just three
Tests. The next best wicket-takers for the team were Sachin
Tendulkar and Zaheer Khan with 3 each! Despite the 'miracle'
that VVS and Dravid pulled off in Kolkata, India would have lost
the series if Bhajji hadn't taken 15 wickets in the deciding match
at Chennai.

I hadn't seen such deadly bowling by an Indian spinner since
Kumble's 10-wicket haul against Pakistan in 1998. With his
jaunty run up and moderate pace bowling, Bhajji extracted mean
bounce and turn from the pitch to have the Aussie batsmen in all
sorts of trouble.

Bhajji wasn't a classical off-spinner in the Erapalli Prasanna
mould, nor was he peculiarly individualistic like Muttiah
Muralitharan. He found his own style and rhythm which served
him well for almost two decades across all formats of the game.
Some critics thought that he didn't flight the ball enough.
Perhaps. But he played to his strengths: powerful fingers that
gave the ball plentiful revs, exploiting any turn and bounce in
the pitch to the fullest, and a deceptive doosra which brought
about the downfall of many.

What I liked about Bhajji was that he never backed away
when conditions were not favourable. I've seen him so often, in

Tests, ODIs and T20s, giving it his all even though everything seemed ranged against him. And it paid off – you can't have 417 Test wickets if you are not good enough.

On the field, he could be a confrontationist, and get under the skin of batsmen. This worked to his and the team's advantage. As a player and captain in my day, I was always wary of those cricketers who lived by niceties to impress those writing in newspapers or doing commentary rather than trying to win the match. In my team, Bhajji would have been an early pick.

He was very underrated as a batsman. With two Test centuries to his credit, he certainly had the potential to contribute more runs.

Between them, Kumble and Bhajji took 1,000-plus Test wickets. It's very difficult for one bowler to take 600-plus wickets if there is no support from the other end. These two complemented each other superbly, and, on Indian pitches, made life hell for visiting batsmen.

GAME CHANGER

Adam Gilchrist

 Adam Gilchrist is an easy selection for any team in any format at any time in the history of the game. His explosive stroke play, clubbed with fine wicketkeeping skills, make him arguably the most influential player of his generation and the greatest wicketkeeper ever.

Australia has traditionally produced wicketkeepers of very high pedigree. Indian players of the 1960s I spoke to rate Wally Grout, who came to the country twice, very highly for his skills on slow, turning pitches with low bounce. In my time, Ian Healy was a constant feature of the Australian side. Healy was not only technically magnificent behind the wickets, but also made important and impactful contributions with the bat. His keeping especially to Shane Warne in his early days gave the young leg spinner a lot of confidence.

Though he might be a little behind Grout and Healy for sheer technique, especially on slow pitches, I would put Gilchrist ahead of the other two simply because of his ability with the bat. As a wicketkeeper, he was top-class, swift of reflex, at times acrobatic, and supremely fit, hardly ever missing a match. But when you attach batting ability to his KRA, he becomes peerless.

In ninety-six Tests, Gilchrist made seventeen Test centuries at an average over 47. These are stats that would be the envy of any top-order, frontline batsman. Add to this his strike rate – 80-plus in Tests – and you get an idea why Australia were such a formidable side in the decade he played.

There were no half measures in Gilchrist's batting. He could make a mockery of any attack on any pitch with his free swing of the bat, playing strokes in front of the wicket like he was teeing off on a golf course. He was unafraid of lofting the ball into the air, which made it difficult to set a field for him.

Gilchrist's attacking batting in the number seven position meant Australia could sustain a high scoring rate till late in the order. It also meant that opponents would frequently find their hopes dashed just when they thought they had things under control.

In the memorable Test series against Australia in 2000-01, which India won 2–1 after a sensational 281 by V.V.S. Laxman in Kolkata and some touch-and-go moments in Chennai, it was in the first Test in Mumbai that Gilchrist shone. His counter-attack, paired splendidly with some big hitting by left-hander Matthew Hayden, turned things around at a time when it seemed like Australia were in deep crisis.

Gilchrist batted in two gears – top and overdrive – and this would leave opponents brutalized. In 2002, at Johannesburg, he changed the course of the match in a little over two hours, scoring 204 at almost a run a ball. In 2006, England were at the receiving end as he made a century off just 57 deliveries, just a ball slower than Viv Richards's then world record. There were plenty of such knocks, some of them cameos, not more than 30 or 40 runs, but vital to the team's cause.

Gilchrist was equally destructive in ODIs, where he opened the innings with Hayden for a large part of his career. They formed as devastating a pair as West Indies's Gordon Greenidge and Desmond Haynes, and played a big role in Australia's three consecutive World Cup wins between 1999 and 2007. Gilchrist scored half-centuries in the 1999 and 2003 semi-finals, and a smashing century in 2007, aided by a golf ball embedded in his batting glove for a better grip.

Some player, Gilly!

ALL-SHOT WONDER

Kumar Sangakkara

Kumar Sangakkara is arguably Sri Lanka's greatest batsman. The small island country has produced an array of dazzling batters: from Roy Dias, Duleep Mendis, Sidath Wettimuny, Ranjan Madugalle, Arjuna Ranatunga, Aravinda De Silva in my playing days to the more recent Sanath Jayasuriya and the gifted Mahela Jayawardene with whom Sangakkara teamed up so brilliantly.

But I'd put Sanga at the top of this tree for two reasons: his phenomenal consistency, and the fact that he also kept wickets for almost a decade of his career, which is a huge burden – both physical and mental – to carry at the international level.

Sanga finished with a Test average of 57.40 runs, outstanding by any yardstick. Critics of modern cricket argue that many batsmen and bowlers have flattering statistics because they have played weak teams like Zimbabwe (now, not earlier) and Bangladesh (earlier, not now) as well as recent entrants like Ireland and Afghanistan. My counter is that players don't choose their opponents. They play against teams that exist in the system at a given point in time. About eight decades ago England and Australia were the only established sides; India, West Indies, South Africa and New Zealand were rookie teams. Likewise, Sri Lanka were minnows when they started in international cricket in 1981.

Where Sanga stands out is in the number of runs and the manner in which he got them against the best teams of his time. This includes centuries in every cricket-playing country, barring the West Indies, where he played only four Tests. A stupendous triple and several double tons – out of thirty-eight Test and twenty-five ODI centuries – reveal his deep hunger for runs, superb batting skills and great stamina, whoever the opposition. Swing and seaming conditions in England and New Zealand pose the biggest challenge to batsmen from the subcontinent. Sanga excelled in both countries.

The turning point in his career was the 192 he got against a high-quality Aussie attack in Hobart in 2007 that almost won Sri Lanka the Test. That's when the harshest critics and former players started seeing him differently. I remember Ian Chappell praising Sanga to the skies for that knock. His stock in international cricket soared thereafter.

What impressed me most was that Sanga, instead of slowing down with age, just seemed to get better and better with every passing year. The decision to give up wicketkeeping in Tests was a wise one, as it allowed him more bandwidth to focus on batting as a top-order player. He wasn't far behind in limited-overs cricket either, and the four successive centuries he made in the 2015 World Cup in the sunset of his career were a remarkable achievement.

Sanga is among the most versatile batsmen I've seen, in any format. His technique was compact and tight, the margin of error reduced significantly because he played so close to his body. He commanded all the strokes in the book, but what I fancied most was the cover drive, played inside out. It could destroy the confidence of any bowler.

The ability to switch from defence to attack, and vice versa, is the hallmark of great players. One requires not only exceptional skill, but also a strong temperament and a knack for reading the trend of play. In this, Sanga was masterly and an education for budding batsmen.

His farewell match was against India, at Colombo in 2015. I don't know why he decided to retire after the second Test and not the end of the series. But the farewell was an occasion to remember, with the then Sri Lankan President Maithripala Sirisena offering him the post of High Commissioner to the UK there and then.

This showed the high stature he held in his own country. In a land torn by strife every now and then, Sanga's was a voice of reason and reconciliation that struck a chord everywhere.

To the surprise of many, Sanga refused the President's offer with apologies. I remember walking up to him after the presentations, congratulating him for his enormous contribution to the game, telling him that he will get ample reward for this soon enough.

In 2019, Sangakkara became the first non-English President of the Marylebone Cricket Club. Nobody deserved it more, for not only was he a great player in his day, but also a statesman for the game.

UNIVERSE BOSS

Chris Gayle

Chris Gayle is an international superstar. With his dreadlocks, wide toothy smile, distinct mannerisms and big hitting, you cannot miss him on a cricket field. I don't know about you, but he sets my pulse racing whenever he is in the middle. He could hit the next ball, or the next six balls, for sixes. Or he might get out, mishitting the very first ball he plays.

Of course, given his track record, the latter situation is highly unlikely. Many bowlers have come to grief believing that Gayle is a hit-or-miss batsman – someone who defies percentages, plays to the gallery, chances his arm and will throw his wicket away. What does happen is that Gayle gets the measure of the pitch quickly and unleashes a couple of boundaries to stamp his authority in the middle. If the bowler is hustled, then he will cut loose, making it impossible for the fielding team to stem the flow of runs. Gayle's renown has come largely from T20 cricket, but his Test record – over 100 matches, fifteen centuries of which two are triple tons, and an average of over 42 – cannot be dismissed. These are fantastic figures for an opening batsman, especially in a team that has been struggling in the five-day format for the past two decades.

It's a shame that his problems with the West Indies cricket administration restricted his Test appearances. Considering the current paucity of high-quality talent in the Caribbean, Gayle could easily have played thirty or forty more Tests and taken his career aggregate to over 10,000 runs.

The recompense for fans is that not playing Tests has stretched and enhanced his career in limited-overs cricket. He is that rare breed of cricketer who has been hugely successful in every format, and a batsman whom bowlers dread. Not unlike Virender Sehwag, but even Viru hasn't had the same success in the shorter formats.

In ODIs and T20s, Gayle has been dazzling and devastating. His power hitting has transformed the white-ball game. He is a match-winner and crowd-puller like none other. Gayle ensures the turnstiles are moving and that the crowds keep coming, which is what every sport needs for sustenance. And it's not his appearance or some theatrics that he indulges in, but what he does with the bat that has captured the imagination of fans. Nobody hits the ball as easily and as frequently over the fence as he does. Past forty, the body's stiffer and footwork less fluid. But if the ball is delivered in his zone, fielders have to travel long distances to fetch it.

There are not too many ways to keep Gayle quiet. He has few off days in white-ball cricket. Spinners who flight the ball with exemplary control draw him forward to play away from the body, or lure him to use his feet and beat him in the air, stand a chance early in his innings. If that doesn't work, the best option is prayer. His batting is based on power and superb eye–hand coordination, and involves minimal use of his feet. His bat must be one of the heaviest logs of wood being used in world cricket. Given his physical stature and large hands, the bat doesn't look too big, but it can send the ball high and far.

Although I have seen many Gayle innings over the years, two stand out for me. One was in South Africa in the inaugural T20 World Championship in 2007. He lit up the tournament with a century against the home team at Wanderers Stadium, hitting more than a dozen sixes. At that point in time, a century in T20 was thought almost impossible, and I remember there was frenzy even in the commentary box at Gayle's furious hitting.

The second knock came twelve years later in the West Indies, when I was coach of the Indian team. This was the nearly forty-year-old's 300th match. There was a lot of talk in the media and the West Indies cricket circles at the time about him retiring. He replied to his critics by smashing the daylights out of us in Port of Spain with a blistering 72 runs.

The power with which he hit that day was unreal. Off the field, he's a great fun. I remember having a few beers with him after that game, and he had us in splits with his wisecracks and mimicry. Like so many people from the Caribbean, he doesn't seem burdened by worry, taking life as it comes.

Nearly two years later, Gayle's still around, smashing bowlers in the various T20 leagues across the world, and showing up for the West Indies in limited-overs cricket, claiming that he might play for another five years! This time sceptics are silent.

I'm an unabashed Gayle fan. His appeal is worldwide, and he's done more to popularize the game than most cricketers of his era, particularly in countries where interest was slackening. This was more pronounced in the Caribbean where cricket's pristine position was under serious threat. He draws in crowds to stadiums and TV screens, and is a sponsor's and broadcaster's dream. There is good reason why he is the most coveted player even today in T20 leagues.

HIGH SKILLS, BIG HEART

Zaheer Khan

 No matter the type of ball – new or old, red or white – Zaheer Khan was an outstanding fast bowler. His great strength was his ability to 'read' batsmen and then set them up to make a mistake. But for injuries, he would surely have finished with 400-plus Test wickets.

I haven't seen a better exponent of reverse swing from India than Zak. Kapil Dev was a maestro who could swing the ball both ways and late. He was classically orthodox, and did not experiment much. In fact, he started doing so with reverse swing only towards the end of his career, when Manoj Prabhakar shared the secret with him!

Zak surpassed even Manoj where reverse swing was concerned. He was quicker through the air and disguised it quite superbly to leave batsmen guessing. How to 'make' a ball for it to swing the 'other way' is one part of the theory; the other, and perhaps the more important part, is concealing which side of the ball is shinier and pitching it at the right length and line to trouble batsmen. Gripping the ball so as to hide it from the view of the batsman while running in to bowl, without appearing self-conscious or awkward, requires experimentation and practice. Smart batsmen are always looking for signs to tell them what a bowler is up to.

Historically, Pakistanis have been most adept at reverse swing. Wasim Akram was the best I've seen in keeping batsmen guessing how his next delivery would behave. Waqar Younis was only a little behind. After they retired, Zak was the best exponent of reverse swing in international cricket for almost a decade.

The best cricketers are eager and quick learners. Starting as a tearaway fast bowler, Zak realized two things: if he couldn't hone his skills to a high degree quickly, and didn't learn how to conserve energy, his career in Indian cricket would be short-lived. On the international circuit, he got the chance to pick the brains of guys like Wasim, but what helped him most was a stint in county cricket.

Being on the county circuit for a couple of years is invaluable education, especially for young cricketers. For reasons I haven't been able to fathom, too few Indian players make use of this opportunity. In a way, the IPL affords young players similar exposure. They brush shoulders with the best cricketers, learn from them the skills and temperament required to survive. But the IPL is only the T20 format; county cricket is still the better learning ground for the longest format of the game.

Zak was a changed cricketer after he played county cricket. He made the shift from being a reasonably good fast bowler into a testing, probing, threatening swing bowler against the best batsmen in the world. In 2007, he was the key figure in India's Test victory over England after twenty-one long years and remained the spearhead of the bowling attack till he retired.

In limited-overs cricket, he enjoyed equal success in this period because he adapted so well to using the white ball. In the 2003 and 2011 World Cups, Zak was India's highest wicket-taker. In fact, in the latter tournament, he bowled three maiden overs and picked up two wickets to start with in the final. He didn't get enough praise for this, though it was instrumental in India winning the title.

He was a very motivated competitor who bowled his heart out in Indian conditions that, till very recently, hardly helped fast bowlers. While Kapil Dev is the fountainhead of India's fast-bowling prowess today, Zaheer Khan, without doubt, has been the one to accelerate the transformation – with Javagal Srinath acting as a vital bridge between the two. And Zak has done this not only by his own performances, but in the mentoring role he took on himself even while playing. In 2007, when I took over briefly as coach (against Bangladesh), I spent some time with Zak and realized the influence he was already wielding over fellow bowlers in the team.

Fast bowling is not an easy task. If you don't love it, you can't do it. Likewise, mentoring is extremely difficult unless you have the personality for it. If you don't enjoy it, you can hardly inspire others with your ideas and skills.

Zak was an out and out competitor, but also a very relaxed human being who didn't stress beyond a point. He loved the game, enjoyed travelling, was comfortable in diverse surroundings and company. An asset on the field, in the dressing room, anywhere really.

As coach of the Indian team, every young fast bowler I've met in the past six or seven years has something to thank Zak for. Any player, young or old, can turn to him for advice at any time. He parts with expertise readily, and with a smile, just as he played his cricket.

DEMOLITION MAN

Virender Sehwag

 Virender Sehwag was unarguably one of the greatest batsmen of the modern era, and someone who entertained fans with his attacking stroke play wherever he went. Most batsmen change their approach as they get older, either to preserve their average or conserve their fitness. Viru changed neither his approach nor his style; he zoomed through his career in top gear.

That he was so successful over such a long period of time made him a great asset for India in every format. He set up more wins than anybody else, at least in the first decade of his career, because of the scorching pace at which he scored. He could pummel the best bowlers into submission in a frontal attack and was dreaded by the best.

To average 49 in Tests, batting the way he did was remarkable. He was a high-risk player for sure, but not a 'maaro ya maro' slogger. His mind was always ticking, looking for opportunities to score and he would work out the success/failure percentage of strokes instinctively. His strike rate – 82.23 in Tests, 104.33 in ODIs and 145.38 in T20 internationals – is extraordinary by any reckoning, and is a testament to his skill. He just enjoyed batting and flaying the leather off the ball gave him even more pleasure than statistical milestones. That is perhaps why he was always humming a song when batting!

Any batsman who hits a Test triple century in his career earns immortality. Viru scored two. He would have got a third too, against Sri Lanka at the Brabourne in 2010, but fell on 293 trying to reach the landmark with a big hit. He had twenty-three centuries in 104 Tests, which is a high conversion rate, and highlights yet again that he was not a slogger.

The first time I saw Viru bat was in Los Angeles in the late 1990s for India A in a tournament organized by Mark Mascarenhas. Conditions in LA were not suited for cricket, but Viru played some superb cameos on dirty tracks, which caught my eye. He seemed different from other players in the same age group. I discovered soon enough just how different when I watched him score a century on his Test debut at Bloemfontein in 2001, robbing me of adjectives as he put up a big partnership with Sachin Tendulkar, matching the maestro stroke for stroke.

There were two major inflection points in Viru's career. The first was soon after his debut century batting number six, when he was promoted to open the innings at a time when India was struggling for stability at the top. Many thought he didn't have the technique to play the new ball, especially when it was swinging. But Viru was never short on self-belief. He made a go of it with smart, percentage cricket and bravado.

The second was the brilliant 195 against Australia at the Melbourne Cricket Ground (MCG) in 2003-04. He had a few centuries to his name by then, but bashing up the Aussie bowlers on the first morning in a Boxing Day Test brought him centre stage in the cricket world, a spot which he wouldn't vacate till the last year or so of his career.

That MCG innings was magnificent. I remember fellow commentators and I getting into breathless description and explanation of Viru's dashing approach, explosive strokes, and finally, his dismissal for 195 trying to reach a double ton with a six! When I look back to that innings, I can't help but marvel at what Viru achieved subsequently. He may have failed to get a double century then, but by the time he finished, eleven of his twenty-three tons were in excess of 150, six went past 200 and two were triple centuries. Mind-boggling!

What made Viru distinctive was eye–hand coordination. He used his hands with more dexterity than any other batsman I've seen in modern cricket. He also had free-flowing arms which allowed him to play all kinds of shots once he had adjusted to line and length. The fact that he chose attack as the best from of defence often brought his technique into question. But what a lot of people forget is that Viru actually had a very sound defence. You can't be a good player off the back foot otherwise. This helped him keep good balls out, yet not let anything loose go unpunished. While his repertoire of strokes was vast, it was Viru's decisiveness that set him apart. He was hardly ever caught in no man's land, was wonderfully inventive, and had the amazing ability to find gaps in the field against fast and slow bowlers.

One of his finest innings was the 293 against Sri Lanka at the Brabourne Stadium in 2009, when he repeatedly cut Muttiah Muralitharan from the leg stump since the onside was packed with fielders. Even the champion off-spinner looked willing to wave the white handkerchief in the face of Viru's assault.

Clarity of thought was his biggest strength on the cricket field. He didn't seem to have any doubt about what he wanted to do. At all times, he was very positive in his mental outlook, and this extended to life outside the field too. I never saw him down in the dumps, whether he made a century or a blob. He'd be whistling at the breakfast table or when taking strike in the middle.

Viru Sehwag was unique. A once-in-a-generation player.

SULTANS OF SWING

James Anderson and Stuart Broad

I consider my contests (as a batsman) against Imran Khan, Ian Botham, Kapil Dev, Wasim Akram, Waqar Younis as among my most memorable and gratifying for the challenges they posed with their late swing. And though I never played against him, just from watching him perform, I think James Anderson could easily be part of this exalted group.

I've observed Anderson from the start of his career, and his evolution from a tearaway fast bowler into a maestro of swing and seam. That he can take wickets on helpful home pitches, as well as on dead-as-dodo tracks in the subcontinent is truly admirable.

The length of Anderson's career is amazing, and is a tribute to both his fitness and skills. He's been playing international cricket for eighteen years now (as I write this), a statistic that finds few parallels among fast bowlers. For all the workload he's carried, the pace at which he still bowls and the control he exercises are remarkable.

Over the years, England has produced some exceptional swing bowlers because of the conditions they grow up in: Brian Statham, Fred Trueman, John Snow and Botham to name a few. Anderson's not only a worthy upholder of this lineage, but easily the best swing bowler from anywhere in the last quarter of a century. In English conditions that are helpful, I'll go a step further and say he's probably been the best of them all.

What makes Anderson so good?

Swing and seam bowling at its best is pure art, no less. It requires nuanced understanding of how to grip the ball, how to hold the seam and wrist in different positions, how much to polish the ball, which side to expose for particular kind of movement, when to release the ball, what line and length to bowl in different conditions and on different pitches. Swing bowling is not just about how much movement one gets. If atmospheric conditions are helpful, banana swing can come easily, but is not necessarily rewarding once batsmen get used to it. It is late movement, often not more than 6–7 inches, that troubles even the best batsmen most.

Anderson has all these qualities and then some. His run up (neither short nor extended), pace (which he can vary from medium to fast), ability to conceal the ball from the batsman's sight (not unlike Akram), final leap and side-on delivery stride are all classical. Taken together, these add up to a sublime expression of talent.

What makes him so successful, though, is a highly competitive and astute mind. Of some spinners, it is said they have the temperament of fast bowlers. Similarly, swing bowlers can have the temperament of spinners: patient, guileful, building up pressure steadily on a batsman, inducing errors by their constant probing through variations in length, line and deviation. Anderson belongs to this category.

He has been able to take so many wickets because his basics are so strong, and because he has improvisations that even the best batsmen struggle to spot early. He is so damn accurate that he will drop the ball on a penny all day. His use of the crease is subtle and smart, control over swing and seam total. He moves the ball both ways and keeps nagging at a batsman's technique or temperament relentlessly, always on the lookout for any weaknesses to exploit.

Like all great bowlers, Anderson's a fine reader of batsmen, and enjoys the 'battle of wits and will' against the best because he has such enormous self-belief in his own abilities. His contests with Virat Kohli in the 2018 Test series in England were memorable because each wanted to dominate the other. This brought out the best in both players, raising the level of play to an enthralling level.

Very early in the series, I remember Virat driving him through the onside. When he walked past him after that, Anderson said to him, 'That's the last such stroke you've played in the series.' And that indeed was the last one, though Virat scored over 500 runs!

When you talk of Jimmy Anderson, you can't not bring Stuart Broad into the conversation. As a combination, they've been absolutely brilliant and have helped each other – and England – superbly from the time they teamed up.

Between them, they have picked up more than 1,000 sticks in Test cricket alone. This is a phenomenal achievement and puts Anderson–Broad in the same league as other great fast bowling pairs who have taken the game to new heights. Think Ray Lindwall and Keith Miller, Brian Statham and Fred Trueman, Wes Hall and Charlie Griffith, Dennis Lillee and Jeff Thomson, Wasim Akram and Waqar Younis, or any combination you may want to choose from the great line-up of pace bowlers the West Indies had in the 1980s and 1990s.

Anderson and Broad differ from each vastly, and while that makes watching them operate in tandem delightful, it also makes life that much more difficult for the batsmen who have to face them. Anderson is a sublime artist, a true-blue master of swing and seam bowling. Broad also gets the ball to swing late and both ways, but because he is considerably taller than his partner, he can get disconcerting bounce and pose a different set of problems. Having to constantly adjust their style against the pair's top-class bowling attack becomes a challenge for even the best batsmen.

Broad's a tough competitor and is always gunning for the batsman. He can go wide of the crease and send a ball thudding into the ribcage of batsmen who are inattentive, nervy or of tardy reflexes. Since he puts a lot more shoulder into his bouncers, these come more quickly off the pitch than batsmen expect.

He is one of those bowlers who can get into spells that decimate batting line-ups. We've seen that against India, and, more tellingly, in a couple of Ashes series played in England. In the 2019 contest between the arch-rivals, he carried the bowling in Anderson's absence with great responsibility.

Broad's most sterling quality is that he's been an avid and constant learner. He does not give up if things don't pan out favourably, as they often do in sport, or rest on his laurels when he's done well. He's just got smarter and better with every match.

I was on the air when Broad was hit for six sixes by Yuvraj Singh in the 2007 T20 World Championship. Not all the deliveries were bad, but that evening, Yuvi was in irrepressible form and I can't think of many bowlers who could have stopped him.

Broad was just twenty-one then. To be roughed up in this manner would have destroyed any bowler's confidence, leave aside a rookie's. Bowlers – pace and spin alike – don't like to be hit freely by batsmen. His comeback since the mauling from Yuvi's bat has been quite remarkable. His batting has come down a notch from his early days, but his bowling's improved substantially, which is what England needed more of.

I played a lot with his father, Chris, who was an opening batsman. I never thought the son would be anything but a batsman because Chris was so obsessed with it, talking technique and discussing other batsmen all the time. I was somewhat surprised when I learnt that Stuart had grown up to be a fast bowler.

What's common between father and son on the field, though, is a short fuse. Chris had a fiery temper and Stuart is not known to hold back when needled. Aggression is in the Broad genes I suppose, but where cricket is concerned, the son has made it count more than his dad.

MR SIXER

Yuvraj Singh

 I was in the commentary box when Yuvraj Singh hit Stuart Broad for six sixes in one over in the inaugural ICC World T20 Championship in 2007. After he hit the third, I told myself, 'Be prepared for something special.' When he hit the fourth, I could almost foresee what would follow.

When I hit six sixes in an over in a first-class match for Mumbai against Baroda many years ago, the first three had been to step up the run-scoring. The fifth and sixth were adventure and ambition riding on an adrenaline rush. The crucial one was the fourth; a hump that had to be overcome with method and measure.

I could sense not only how pumped up Yuvi must have been after hitting that fourth six, but also how downcast young Broad, then only twenty-one, would have been. Tilak Raj, whom I hit for six sixes, put his best effort in the fourth delivery. Once that sailed out of the park, his shoulders sagged, the psychological battle was lost, and the next two deliveries were bowled by a shell-shocked zombie. It was much the same with poor Broad.

Not many players have hit six sixes in an over in any format and, if I may brag a bit, for those who have, the thrill and satisfaction of doing so remains for a lifetime. Yuvi, till then a fantastic batsman, became an icon as he achieved this in an international tournament.

I started calling him 'Junior' after that scintillating innings, and he started addressing me as 'Senior'. In the decade and more since, our camaraderie has extended beyond the six-hitting record we share. Yuvi is an easy-going, flamboyant character and our fondness for similar things has made our relationship not just hassle-free, but pleasurable.

There is also history attached to the relationship. Yuvi's father, Yograj Singh, and I made our Test debut in the same match in New Zealand in 1981, and became very good friends. Yograj was a strongly built fast bowler, who should have played much longer for India. Unfortunately, some ill luck and a fiery temperament, which often saw him at odds with authority, cost him an extended run in the national team.

But Yograj was determined to make his sons represent the country, and, of the two boys, Yuvi showed the promise and desire to go beyond just playing cricket as a hobby. I would hear stories about young Yuvi from fellow first-class players from the north and Makarand Waingankar, journalist and talent scout for several state associations, who was also their family friend.

Initially, the reports were more about how tough Yograj was on his son, how hard he made him train, but gradually I began to hear about how Yuvi was beginning to blossom into a well-built, attacking player with a wide range of powerful strokes and a swagger that was more pronounced than even his father's.

A part of Yuvi's journey as a junior cricketer has been captured in the movie on M.S. Dhoni. Even at that level, he was feared in his age group. He was seen as a star and behaved like one. Tall and rangy, he had a strong physical presence and abundant talent.

From the time he donned India colours, Yuvi became an instant hit with his dashing batting and brilliant fielding. A high backlift and follow-through also made him attractive to watch. Strong arms and shoulders helped him pack great punch in his strokes. Off the front foot especially, he'd lean into the strokes, putting his full weight into them to leave fielders gaping. For the sheer power he exhibited, I'd put him in the Gordon Greenidge, Vivian Richards and Kapil Dev category.

In his heyday, Yuvi was a tremendous crowd-puller. His ability to hit sixes was quite remarkable. He had an easy swing that would send the ball a long distance. This made him extremely popular with fans and the dread of bowlers. When in full flow, he was a real entertainer.

Yuvi's slow bowling abilities were underestimated. As he showed in the 2011 World Cup, he was canny and controlled, probing batsmen all the time. I don't think he ever wanted to be a bowler, but evolved into one because the team needed someone to trundle a few overs. The 'pie chucker', as he got to be known, started having fun doing this and ended up becoming India's MVP in the 2011 World Cup largely because of his bowling.

Sadly, this was also the time he was diagnosed with cancer, and while he survived the disease doughtily, medication and the prolonged treatment seemed to take a toll on his fitness. He was never the same superb natural athlete again and his career tapered off prematurely.

Given his talent, Yuvi's Test record is perhaps a little disappointing. But in ODIs, he was absolutely brilliant. If I had to pick an all-time great side in this format, I would choose Yuvraj Singh unhesitatingly.

MR 360 DEGREES

A.B. de Villiers

Along with Virat Kohli, A.B. de Villiers is the world's best batsman across all three formats I've seen in the past decade or so. Like Virat, ABD's genius is not only in the quality of stroke play and capacity to score runs consistently, but also his versatility. Both men can switch between Test and limited-overs cricket, and between ODIs and T20s with ease. Where most batsmen show stress and strain in making technical adjustments for different formats, Virat and ABD do it almost subliminally, settling quickly into rhythm, and scoring heavily to leave opponents fretting and fuming.

Playing together for the Royal Challengers Bangalore has helped them both grow in stature as batsmen. The IPL is a T20 league, but when you spend so much time together, on and off the field, conversations and discussions will undoubtedly extend to other formats and experiences in the sport. Both Virat and ABD have benefited enormously from being teammates.

I first saw ABD in South Africa during a commentary assignment for SuperSport. He was among the young batsmen coming into the national team then. Hashim Amla was another, and in South African cricketing circles, both were being hailed as batsmen with a great future.

It did turn out as expected, but, at that time, neither ABD nor Hashim were able to make a great start to their Test careers. Frankly, my first impression of ABD wasn't very good. He was obviously a terrific athlete while fielding and running between the wickets. I learnt that he was a multi-discipline sportsman; he even fenced! However, as a batsman, he looked loose, jumpy and vulnerable.

When I saw him a couple of years later though, there had been a remarkable transformation in ABD's batting. In place of the gawky young man with a jack-in-the-box approach was a well-rounded, secure, consummate batsman, who could take bowlers apart with a mix of classical and improvised stroke play.

Not having read or heard about it, I don't know if something specific had triggered the change in him. I think it was more the experience of international cricket, learning from others, and hard work in the nets that helped ABD vault himself to a higher level of batsmanship. Plus, of course, the desire to be recognized among the best.

Such ambition is often overlooked by pundits and critics, when in fact, it plays a big role in how careers are shaped. Players aspire for greatness, setting benchmarks for themselves with those from the past, and compete intensely with their own contemporaries for top honours. I've realized this even more after retiring, and particularly after becoming a coach and interacting with young players from all over the world.

By the time ABD was a few years into international cricket, leading batsmen like Rahul Dravid, Sachin Tendulkar, V.V.S. Laxman, Ricky Ponting, Matthew Hayden, Graeme Smith, Inzamam-ul-Haq, Younis Khan and Mohammad Yousuf were approaching the end of their glittering careers. A void was opening up at the top, and the likes of ABD, Hashim and Kevin Pietersen – to name just three – were among the more gifted prospects aiming to fill it.

ABD's exploits hardly need statistical detailing. These are too well known. The impact and influence he's had on his team, his own country and elsewhere, on budding cricketers the world over, and the legacy he will leave behind are invaluable.

His '360-degree' batting has captivated fans. Like Viv Richards in his heyday, ABD can make a mockery of the bowling with his sheer all-round game. He might not have the brute power of Chris Gayle, but when it comes to 'manipulating' the field, there has been no one better.

His maturity shone in the way he adapted to Test cricket after some initial hiccups, and became selective in his shotmaking. When you have the ability to come up with three shots for the same ball, it can be a problem. Some very gifted batsmen were guilty of profligacy and failed to fulfil their potential.

ABD's consistency shows he did not take his talent for granted. He's got several match-saving innings to his credit, including a heroic one against India when they toured South Africa in 2013. In 2015, playing in India, he and Hashim batted dourly for hours, determined to save the match. Ultimately, they couldn't, but their intent, temperament and skills as they batted on a wearing turner were remarkable.

In white-ball cricket, ABD's batting, especially in the slog overs, takes one's breath away. You expect something extraordinary from him, and invariably, he delivers. His biggest asset is anticipation; it's almost as if his sixth sense tells him what the bowler will be attempting which allows him to make the adjustments to target an untenanted part of the field. In this aspect, he is unique.

It's a pity that ABD gave up on Test cricket so early. I was surprised when he announced his decision. He was in peak form and fitness, and looked good for at least 3,000–4,000 runs more, which would have put him among the best of the best.

Looking back, I think it was mistake to saddle him with the captaincy. In South African cricket, this responsibility sits better on guys like Graeme Smith and Faf du Plessis, who are thicker-skinned and can absorb the pressure better. ABD had so much to do with bat and in the field – including frequently keeping wickets – that he shouldn't have been burdened further.

Apart from being a magnificent batsman, ABD has been a great ambassador for cricket: one of those players who will not have a line uttered against him by any of his peers, teammates or opponents, which speaks volumes of his character and the way he played the sport.

ACE OF PACE

Dale Steyn

Dale Steyn steaming in from his full run up, wicketkeeper standing deep, four or five slip catchers in place, match in the balance – this rates among the most thrilling sights in international cricket. Technically and aesthetically, he was in the same category as Dennis Lillee and Richard Hadlee – and matched their mean desire to take wickets.

Steyn had a superb action and fantastic skills that could not be suppressed by conditions and pitch. Like Lillee and Hadlee in their heyday, Steyn could induce pin-drop silence in the stadium or raise the excitement to a crescendo, depending on whether he was playing at home or away. Rival dressing rooms would be on tenterhooks, irrespective of where the match was being staged.

I saw a lot of Steyn in South Africa in the first decade of this century when I was a regular in the SuperSport commentary team. He looked like the perfect athlete who could have excelled in any sport. Fortunately, he chose cricket, and embellished it as few fast bowlers have done.

From his very early days, he looked a match-winner, bowling at a scorching pace, with a superb natural outswinger, and an equally deadly delivery that held its line. I also saw in him the mean and relentless desire for success that typifies great fast bowlers.

With experience, Steyn added more ammo to his arsenal and became even more difficult for batsmen to handle. Apart from raw pace, he now had deceptive bouncers, late swing and reverse swing, and bowled with supreme control. His appetite for wickets had become gluttonous.

Steyn's biggest strength was he could win games from tough positions. The batting side would be chugging along comfortably, and then suddenly, in a short, sizzling burst, he would wreak havoc on their side, turning the game upside down. I remember a post-lunch spell in Nagpur in 2010 when he cleaned up India, taking 7–51. The ball had started reversing a bit, Steyn smelt blood, ran in to bowl even faster, got the ball to move in the air at high pace and the Indian innings was soon in tatters.

At the Wanderer's in 2013, playing against India, Steyn had his tail up, and Rohit Sharma simply couldn't put bat to ball. Not for want of trying, it was just that Steyn was in unplayable form. Of course, Rohit then was not the batsman he would become some years later, but he was still a gifted batsman, among the best in India.

Steyn could wreck strong batting line-ups with ease, and he did this not once or twice, but so often that he became the most successful and feared fast bowler in his prime. In South Africa, he would get wickets rapidly, and without conceding too many runs, which made him the most valuable player of his team, besides Jacques Kallis.

He was not just a giant at home though. His numbers in Australia, India and England are splendid, and one of the main reasons why South Africa had such a fine record overseas too. Even when he cut down on his run up later in his career, Steyn could bowl full throttle – supported by strong shoulder, back and leg muscles – to surprise batsmen with pace and bounce.

I always fancied him in Test matches rather than in limited-overs cricket. He was hugely successful in ODIs and T20s too, but the best expression of his skills and natural aggression came in the longest format of the game. Over a ninety-three-Test career Steyn picked up 439 wickets with a strike rate better than Waqar Younis's and Malcolm Marshall's. What better validation of his capabilities can there be?

For me, he was South Africa's best fast bowler bar none. Allan Donald, Shaun Pollock, Makhaya Ntini belong to a league of excellent fast bowlers from South Africa, especially since the team's return to international cricket. But Steyn is numero uno.

ALL-FORMAT FORCE

Hashim Amla

I first saw Hashim Amla in his debut series in India and wasn't terribly impressed. The high backlift and a seemingly predetermined trigger movement from the stance were not signs of a batsman who would last too long. At the international level, bowlers and opposing captains are quick to spot even the slightest vulnerability.

I thought Hashim would struggle on the slow, turning pitches of the subcontinent (which he did in his first series), as well as in England where the ball swings late or can seam devilishly off the pitch all day. Batsmen with high backlifts can be delayed coming down on the ball. Moreover, it needs a still head and sure footwork to counter lateral movement.

Not that batsmen with high backlifts haven't excelled in such conditions. Zaheer Abbas made tons of runs for Pakistan on home pitches and in England, as did Mohammad Azharuddin for India. They were so full of strokes, stylish and difficult to control largely because they played the ball late, the bat coming down from way above their shoulders.

Both Zed and Azhar, however, possessed excellent footwork from their very early days. Hashim's footwork looked jumpy when he first came to India in 2004. This made his defensive technique seem particularly disorganized. But within a few years, he showed my first impressions about him were flawed with his heavy run making.

Hashim was not a tearaway success. It took him a while to settle into the game. But once he had made minor technical adaptations, he flowered into a truly brilliant batsman. For a couple of years at least, he was easily among the top three in the world, and clearly among the best in South Africa's cricket history.

What I had originally believed to be Hashim's shortcoming – the high backlift – was to become the woe of bowlers all over the world. His footwork was never in the classical mould, like Sunil Gavaskar, Sachin Tendulkar, Gordon Greenidge or Jacques Kallis. But all great batsmen don't necessarily have to become exemplars of coaching manual prescriptions. The key to successful batsmanship is to be able to play through the line consistently, except in horizontal strokes like the hook, pull, cut.

For these, batsmen have to make their own individual adjustments to reach a degree of comfort playing pace or spin, and on all kinds of pitches. This requires hard work in the nets, a mind that seeks lessons from others through constant self-analysis. One doesn't excel at the highest level just like that. It requires a lot of effort, physical and mental, and loads of ambition.

Once Hashim had worked out the technique that suited him best, he fast-tracked into eminence. Tensile wrists and crisp timing – like Zed, Azhar and V.V.S. Laxman – made his strokes, played a nanosecond later than most batsmen, beautiful to watch.

What impressed me about Hashim's batting was not just the delectable quality and wide repertoire of strokes, but also his temperament. He could adapt quickly to different pitches and bowling attacks without making it seem onerous. This made him an extremely versatile batsman. His patience and diligence helped him score over 500 runs in the 2010 series in India, 300 in an innings in England, while fasting, and a blistering century in Australia, all within a year and a half. Unsurprisingly, on home pitches, he was a master.

Alongside his fantastic run in Tests, Hashim was highly prolific in ODIs too. In fact, for a longish period he was perhaps the best in the world in this format as he reeled off centuries with assembly line production regularity. When T20 cricket arrived, some believed he would be a misfit in a format which put a premium on power strokes. But he left critics dumbfounded with his ability to improvise or invent strokes which made the scorebook dance with runs against his name.

The value of Hashim's batting for his team was in the momentum he created. Unless circumstances demanded attrition, he scored runs – from the start of an innings – at a tempo that kept taking the game forward, creating the opportunity for his team to win.

His form sadly dipped in his last few years in the game. Having followed South Africa's cricket for a long time, I thought captaincy was an unnecessary burden on Hashim. It drained him mentally. He felt the pressure acutely, which resulted in failures, and a consequent sense of non-fulfilment that lingered on even after he surrendered the captaincy.

Like Gundappa Viswanath, Hashim is an extremely likable man, but too nice a bloke to be captain. You need thick skin and cussedness to succeed in the top job. In his case, it must have been even more difficult considering the societal and cricket system as it exists in South Africa.

While his record as captain is unimpressive, as batsman, Hashim Amla was a delight, a class apart and among the greatest batsmen in his country.

GREAT CAREER, INTERRUPTED

Kevin Pietersen

It's a matter of regret for cricket that Kevin Pietersen's career was truncated when he was still at his peak. He was good for at least 2,000 Test runs more when he fell afoul of England's cricket administration.

I don't have sufficient information to sit in judgement on who was wrong in the developments that unfortunately led to him losing his place. That Pietersen did not get unanimous support from within the dressing room itself suggests that the turmoil ran deep, and does not show him in a complimentary light.

However, in my experience, some sportspersons can be strongly individualistic, even maverick in their ways, as several examples across disciplines attest. Those in authority need to understand this, especially in team sports where the emphasis is on interpersonal relationships. As a former captain and present coach, I have found that such players can be tackled with a show of authority or empathy, depending on the personality or the situation. The key is to know which approach to use with whom and when. A mismatch or a mix and match can go haywire.

Big blokes with a strut and a swagger might exude bravado, but can also be fragile and insecure, unsure of where they stand in the scheme of things. Sometimes, matters can precipitate into a severe crisis so swiftly that things get out of whack. Timing, as on the field, becomes as important off the field in these situations. From an outsider's perspective, I would say that the administration and Pietersen could have both been a little more respectful towards each other, and tried to resolve the crisis, rather than stoke it to breaking point.

I am discussing this at some length because what was lost to the game, consequently, was a supremely gifted player, a match-winner in any format, and a great entertainer who drew in big crowds everywhere.

Pietersen's urge and ability to dominate bowlers made him different from typical English batsmen. In fact, this went against his South African pedigree too. A bristling, confrontationist approach on the field of play made him more like an Aussie, intent on winning every battle, with words or with bat. His body language in the middle and readiness for a scrap made him a feared opponent. But it wasn't so much the aggressive approach that made him so successful; rather, how well he allied this to his fantastic talents.

His counter-attacking 186 on a turning track at Mumbai in second Test of the 2013 series after 2 early wickets had fallen was nothing short of genius. England had lost the first Test at

Ahmedabad; another defeat could have finished the contest and perhaps led to a whitewash by India.

Pietersen decided, quite rightly, that the only way to survive was to take the attack to the spinners. He did so with audacity and breathtaking strokes. Three things stood out for me in that innings. For such a big man, Pietersen was very light on his feet, which messed up the length of the spinners. He was also innovative, unafraid to play the reverse sweep or making width to cut deliveries on the stumps on a tricky pitch, unlike players from the past who would have been trying to win the contest through orthodox technique. This can buy you time, but not get enough runs to win a match on turners. The third and, in the context of this match, most important thing was his ability to clear the field, as power hitting can put spinners off their length and demoralize them. These strokes obviously come loaded with risk. It takes gumption to play them.

What helped Pietersen was not just the strength in his arms and back, but also his legs. This gave him the balance needed to play those attacking shots. Without such mooring, the probability of a mishit enhances. Pietersen's 186 was among the best innings by an overseas player I've seen. I'd put it even ahead of Viv Richards's 109 not out at Delhi in 1987. In counter-attacking prowess there was not much to choose between the two, except England were already 1 down in the 2013 series; hence, the hardship factor was greater.

This was not the first time Pietersen had helped England to a stunning upset victory. He was among the central figures in the 2005 Ashes win, when he established himself as a world-class batsman, capable of decimating the best bowling attacks. As he grew in stature and experience, he also became a marvellous improviser. The switch hit, which he introduced in the sport, was awesome in its concept as well as in the timing and power he could bring to it.

Being England's best batsman put him up for the leadership job, as generally happens. But sometimes, when such supremely talented guys are given the captaincy, it may not work out quite as well as anticipated. As a captain you have to put yourself in every player's shoes. This can be quite a complex situation, for not all players are equal in talent and temperament. It demands steady thinking and a thorough understanding of fellow players, their tribulations and frailties, which may not come so easily to go-getters and self-starters.

This may have been a shortcoming in Pietersen's captaincy. As I mentioned, this is not easy to judge from the outside. Whenever we've met, I've found him personable, lively and stimulating.

The big blow was not Pietersen losing the captaincy as much as cricket losing Pietersen.

BACK

IN THE

DRESSING

ROOM,

DIFFERENT

AVATAR

CAPTAIN COOLEST

Mahendra Singh Dhoni

Shortly after the third Test at Melbourne in 2014 was drawn, Mahendra Singh Dhoni made his decision to retire from Test cricket known in the dressing room. The silence could've been cut with a knife. Not a single player so much as shuffled their feet for a while. My jaw hit the floor.

It was surreal. Midway through the series, one of India's greatest players and most successful captains just walks in and announces that he's had enough, and is quitting the scene – and there isn't even a flicker of tension on his face! What should one do?

MS was India's, in fact the world's, biggest player then with three ICC trophies under his belt, including two World Cups, and some very impressive silverware from the IPL. His form was good, and he was just ten matches shy of completing 100

Tests. Still one of the top-three fittest players on the team, he would have the opportunity to boost his career stats if nothing else. True, he wasn't getting any younger, but he wasn't *that* old either! His decision just didn't make sense.

All cricketers say landmarks and milestones don't matter, but some do. I approached the issue in a roundabout way, probing for an opening to make him change his mind. But there was a firmness to MS's tone that stopped me from pushing the matter any further. Looking back, I think his decision was correct; also brave and selfless.

I had wondered then if he might have regrets after some time had passed, but MS has been a revelation. He was still captain in the ODIs and T20s, still a huge influence in Indian cricket, but never once let this impinge on what the players did, or how they settled in with new Test captain Virat Kohli. Giving up on the most powerful position in cricket in the world, in a way, couldn't have been easy.

There are always doubts about how a senior player, and a hugely successful former captain at that, will fit in with youngsters and a new captain. But MS's conduct in the years that followed was exemplary, even more so after he quit the ODI and T20 captaincies as well. He gelled superbly – as a fellow player, advisor, mentor, bulwark – as the situation demanded. This earned him even more respect from seniors and juniors alike, and showed his mature understanding of player and dressing-room dynamics.

MS's impact on Indian cricket has been enormous. As a player, he is in the same league as Sachin Tendulkar and Kapil Dev where multi-format excellence is concerned. (Virat Kohli, if he sustains form for the next few years, will be included in this club, but I can't think of a fourth right now.) Yet, this hardly looked likely when he first came on the international scene.

My earliest memories of him are from late 2004. There had been a buzz about an exciting twenty-four-year-old stroke player from Ranchi, but this was hardly in evidence when he made 0, 12 and 7 not out in his first three matches. As it is, former players are generally wary – and sometimes cynical – when they hear that so-and-so young player is the next big star. One can understand the enthusiasm of people who support such players, but few make it big.

After three flops in succession against Bangladesh, MS failed in his fourth match too. This was against Pakistan, always an emotive issue with Indian fans and sometimes selectors, so the question being asked among us commentators as to whether he belonged at this level or not was not misplaced. MS somehow retained the faith of the selectors for the next match against Pakistan and smashed 148. Overnight, fan emotions and the opinion of commentators had turned in his favour. By the time the year was through, he had thrashed Sri Lanka for an unbeaten 183.

The Dhoni era had begun.

For almost a decade after, our paths crossed frequently, but MS and I hardly got to know each other. Though we focused on the same sport and were at the same matches, he had his job to do and I had mine. But I watched his rapid growth with interest and admiration. His unflappable temperament was something that bemused me at first, then amazed me as I realized it wasn't put on, but in fact his strength of character.

Nothing frazzled him. In the tightest of situations, in defeat or victory, he would be as solidly steadfast and unemotional as a practicing monk. 'Captain Cool' is something of a cliché now, but in many ways, still the most apt description for MS. The only time I saw a flicker of disappointment on his face was after we lost the semi-final of the 2019 World Cup to New Zealand. I could almost see a tear in his eye, of self-admonishment, that he should have been run out when so much depended on him.

As Team Director during 2014–16, and then as chief coach from mid-2017, I got to know MS better. Being in the same dressing room gave me greater insight into the player and the man, and, in both aspects, he is top-class. He has respect for even the most junior player and is never demeaning while offering criticism. His teammates respected him for that even after he had given up the captaincy.

MS is an unorthodox cricketer. His technique, in front of and behind the stumps, is not easily replicable. My suggestion to youngsters is don't try imitating him unless it comes naturally. What made him so successful were his splendid hands. They were quicker than a pickpocket's! No other wicketkeeper, at least in the era MS has played, was that fast. He was the best in the world for a long while, and in white-ball cricket by a long distance.

MS was sharp in his observation of whatever was happening on the field, and uncanny when it came to taking decisions based on 'reading' the trend of play. This quality of his went unnoticed simply because he made such few mistakes. His success with the Decision Review System shows not just fine judgement, but also how well he would be positioned behind the stumps to make the call.

As a batsman, his technique was distinct. In tough circumstances, he would show steel and staying power, but otherwise had an aggressive approach which put bowlers under pressure. The helicopter shot was unique in its intent and execution. To scoop a yorker or even a half-volley over the onside boundary demands a great eye, tremendous bat speed, and a lot of power in the wrists and forearms. He made it look routine.

As an individual too, MS is an unusual man. He is reserved and keeps his thoughts largely to himself. His ability to insulate himself from all the brouhaha that surrounds cricket in India has been quite remarkable. Sharp and astute, he can cut through the clutter – whether on cricketing matters or otherwise – and reach decisions swiftly. (Sometimes, the decision can be astounding, leaving people scratching their heads!)

From his humble beginnings in Ranchi, Mahendra Singh Dhoni became cricket's biggest drawcard for more than a decade, and a massive inspiration for youngsters in India, especially from the hinterland. The legacy he leaves behind is unmatched.

KANE IS ABLE

Kane Williamson

Kane Williamson is a remarkable player and captain. Though he made a hundred on Test debut, for the first few years of his career, he looked a batsman fit only for the longest format of the game. But he's been able to adjust since, shift gears, and make a huge impact in limited-overs cricket too.

The 2019 World Cup, where he carried New Zealand's hopes as batsman and captain to almost clinch the trophy, has been the high point of his cricketing life so far. In the end – though England won the title, somewhat fortuitously I might add, hardly anybody who saw that final believes New Zealand deserved to lose. This is largely due to the composure shown by Williamson in a contentious climax decided by a rule that everybody in hindsight agreed was ludicrous.

I can't think of any other captain keeping his cool after such a result. Playing in a final gets every player's adrenaline pumping, especially the captain's, and to see the coveted trophy slip out of grasp on what was really a technicality, would have shattered a lesser man.

For Williamson to appear so measured and without any rancour seeing the Cup go to Eoin Morgan was extraordinary. Like England, New Zealand too have never won the World Cup, and this would have been a bitter pill for the Kiwi captain to swallow. The force of his personality shone during the post-match functions. Williamson kept his emotions in check, serving as an example to cricketers – especially youngsters – all over the world. I put it on social media then that he was 'Kane and able', which wasn't just a play on words, but my admiration for him.

In the semi-final against India, Williamson had stood out, both as batsman and captain. He dropped anchor after two early wickets, helped his side to a reasonable score, and then inspired his bowlers and fielders to defend it tooth and nail. The match was spread over two days because of rain. It wouldn't have been easy for Williamson and the New Zealand team to live through the anxiety of what was likely to happen the next day. Most people expected us to win comfortably, but we knew that conditions would help the bowlers, and batting would be difficult. Williamson made it doubly difficult by attacking us, instead of waiting for the batsmen to make mistakes.

He was severely tested when M.S. Dhoni, Hardik Pandya and Ravindra Jadeja brought us back into the game after the top order had crashed. It was a tense match in which leadership during the run chase was critical. Bowling changes and field placings had to be well thought out to maintain pressure on the batsmen. Most importantly, Williamson had to have the self-belief to win. As it turned out, not only did he have the belief, he passed it on to his team who withstood the Indian challenge with aplomb. MS's run-out by a direct throw from Martin Guptill, showed how keen and primed New Zealand were to win. MS rarely gets run out. He failed by a couple of centimetres and that was the end of our campaign.

I have followed Williamson's career with interest ever since his young days. He made a fine impression as an Under-19 player, and is one of those cricketers who has not only lived up to the early promise, but exceeded it by miles. He might look the calmest on the circuit, but he has a raging desire to succeed. In that, he is very much in the Rahul Dravid mould: no histrionics, no playing to the gallery, just deep resolve to go out into the middle and do his best, actualize his potential.

He has solid technique – compact, tight, correct – and also a vast range of strokes which he plays with finesse, relying more on timing and placement than on power, which makes him very pleasing to the eye. Punched drives off the back foot on either side are highlights of his batting. These are not easy shots to play. Getting into position quickly requires nimble footwork, beating the field needs splendid timing and the ability to pick gaps. Williamson does it with aplomb.

I still rate my late friend Martin Crowe as the best Kiwi batsman I've seen, but Williamson is within striking distance of Martin. By the time he finishes playing, he should have broken all batting records for New Zealanders. Why, he might be a threat to those from other countries too. He's a special player, destined for special things.

MAVERICK

Steve Smith

Steve Smith is the new millennial batting maestro. His ability to score runs heavily anywhere in the world marks him as special. Once he's got his eye in, opponents have to pay a heavy price, for he's almost impossible to contain.

He's got a technique all of his own. I've never seen a top-order batsman move around so much in the crease. The closest I can think of is Javed Miandad. But that had more to do with the way Miandad used the bat – nudges, pushes, jabs and other stuff – rather than feet movement.

Smith's footwork is unique. He can go from leg-stump guard to outside the off stump and whip the ball to mid-wicket, leaving the bowler and fielders bewildered. And while onlookers have their hearts in their mouths watching him, he rarely misses a ball! This can be terribly disorienting for the opposing team, as all bowling plans can go *phut*. Initially, there were some snide observations about Smith's unusual technique, but these were quashed by the tall scores he kept quickly accumulating. Ultimately, what matters in this game is how many runs a batsman makes.

Purity of technique, grace and style are extremely important in their own way, yet secondary to the volume of runs. The truly great batsmen are identified by their consistent high scoring, and this requires more than just technical virtuosity. There are many batsmen of excellent ability whose achievements have remained modest because their ambition did not match their talent. On the other hand, some less-gifted players have been hugely successful because of their tough-minded approach.

I first saw Smith in action when Australia came to India in 2013. I'd heard of him a couple of years earlier, but as a leg spinner who could bat a bit. Imagine my surprise when, in the third Test in Mohali, he walked out at number five. His credentials as a batsman were still very limited then, but in a daunting situation (Australia had already lost the first two Tests), after he had gotten over the initial heebie-jeebies, Smith settled down to make a fine 92.

When I saw him again, in the 2014 series Down Under, I had moved from the commentary box to the dressing room as Team Director. In this rubber, two batsmen shifted gears in their careers, moving towards greatness: Virat Kohli and Steve Smith. Before the first Test, Smith was a subject of discussion in our team meetings, but not the central theme. By the time the series ended, how to keep Smith quiet was the only issue we discussed.

In the series in India in 2017, Smith's bat produced runs by the ton. On turning pitches, this was a remarkable performance.

India is not the only country to have suffered at Smith's hands. From 2014-15 he's been a thorn in the flesh for all teams, and at every level. In the 2019 Ashes series, he was sensational. Coming back after a one-year ban for ball tampering, he showed no sign of nerves. On the contrary, he displayed amazing strength of mind and will to plunder, amassing more than 700 runs. His average of over 60 in Tests inspires awe, but Smith is equally prolific in ODIs. His century in the semi-final of the 2015 World Cup was instrumental in Australia winning the title.

Bowlers around the world have tried to come up with different tactics to thwart his run-scoring, but Smith always has an answer. Even when on the move while batting, his eye–hand coordination is superb. He's got great hands, and an obsessive hunger to keep churning out runs.

In both informal and formal discussions, several past and current players, particularly bowlers, have said that at some stage his unorthodox technique will be his stumbling block. But so far, Smith is holding all the aces.

JADDU AND THE ASHTRONAUT

Ravichandran Ashwin and Ravindra Jadeja

 Ravichandran Ashwin was the toast of the 2020-21 season. No other cricketer performed better than him in Test cricket in that period. For us, he was magnificent with the ball, and not too far behind with the bat. His contributions in the singular triumph in Australia, and then against England were quite simply magnificent.

Ashwin is a super intelligent guy. My term of endearment for him is 'Ashtronaut'. Talk to him for just a few minutes, and you'll realize his wavelength is different. It's always broadband! He's a qualified engineer with an inquiring bent of mind, and he's always working on some new theory to get batsmen out or to score runs. He can spend hours–days–weeks working on his skills and game plans. This is his strength, but sometimes also his weakness, especially when it comes to batting. A strong grounding in technique and the capacity to concentrate for long periods of time are good enough to score runs consistently without trying to do something special every time.

Ashwin's a genuine all-rounder. In the 2020-21 season, when his batting abilities were put to searching scrutiny, he displayed exceptional fighting spirit and defensive technique in Australia; against England at home, he took the bowling apart to score a century that left the opposing team on a ventilator. With five Test centuries to his name already, there is hardly need for further testimony to his batting ability. To have someone like him walk out at number six or number seven is a great boon to the team.

As a spin bowler, Ashwin is from the top drawer. Very few have the skills he has shown. On helpful pitches, he can make the ball talk. In the last few years, with the benefit of experience, he's become technically more sound and far more confident in challenging batsmen even on overseas tracks.

Ashwin in Australia in 2020-21 was very different from the Ashwin in Australia in 2018. This was evident from the way the ball came out of his hand, the angles he used for flight and deception in the air, and the lengths he landed to put batsmen like Steve Smith to serious test. He used the 2020 lockdown period to enormous advantage, drawing on memories of 2018 and working hard in his daily drill to find the right length for Australian pitches. Without the burden of playing competitive cricket, there was time to hone his skills and do ample homework for the challenges he would face Down Under.

Ambition alone is not enough to succeed, though. One must put in continuous effort in the nets to keep improving as a bowler. Credit goes to Ashwin for devoting countless hours to work on how he would bowl in Australia this time. It couldn't have been easy in the middle of a pandemic. Rather than proving his critics wrong, I think it was the desire to prove something to himself that kept him going in this tough phase. There was a discernible change in his bowling approach. The front foot stride was shorter and the transfer of weight far better. This allowed him more scope to get drift, a crucial weapon when there is not much turn in the pitch.

Ashwin was also mentally tougher than before. He'd worked on plans for the top-order batsmen which he shared with the team management before the tour began and kept developing as the tour wore on. It was a roller-coaster series, and I saw him become more competitive, working even more intensely on control and tactics. It made an enormous difference in the series. To outbowl Nathan Lyon on Australian pitches was a great achievement, and reconfigured the pecking order among spinners. Ashwin is a thinking cricketer, always looking to improve. If he continues in this fashion, I am confident he will top the magnificent milestone of 500 Test sticks.

Ravindra Jadeja is an absolute natural. A technically sound batsman and lethal bowler with superb ball sense, he is a genuine all-rounder, always in the thick of the action – batting, bowling or fielding. Among the Indian cricketers I've played with, he reminds me of Kapil Dev and Laxman Sivaramakrishnan. Like them, Jaddu can do astonishing things on the field without showing any stress or strain.

His personality is in complete contrast to Ashwin's. Jadeja isn't one for deep conversation, but he's very intelligent in a different sort of way, and particularly when it comes to cricket. Initially, he seemed stubborn about what he wanted to do, but of late, he's broken out of his comfort zone and become a far better cricketer for it.

In my conversations with him in the last couple of years, I've seen his eagerness to grow technically and tactically. He's more aware of his bowling and batting potential, and what he owes to himself and the team. Discussions about his game with me, the support staff and senior players are more purposeful, and more pertinently, he's receptive if some flaws are highlighted.

The turning point in Jadeja's growth as an all-rounder was his 77 against New Zealand in the 2019 World Cup. Though we lost the match, his sparkling, gutsy knock ensured that it was not by a large margin. This boosted his self-belief as a batsman and he's not looked back since.

In Australia, before injury cut short his tour, he showed excellent form in white- and red-ball cricket. The half-century (57) he scored in December 2020 in Melbourne during the second Test was crucial in helping us level the series and turn the momentum in our favour.

All-rounders have an advantage in that they have multiple opportunities to succeed. Some potential all-rounders are content in doing well in just one aspect. But that is selling yourself short and abdicating your responsibility. The best players rise above this pitfall. Jadeja takes on every task with deadly seriousness and wants to succeed in everything he does.

His strengths as a bowler are pinpoint accuracy and the pace at which he bowls. This gives batsmen very little margin for error. On helpful pitches, he can 'kill' batsmen with turn and bite interspersed with ripping arm deliveries. As a batsman, he's got the natural elegance of left-handers. For some reason, he distrusted his own batting ability – despite multiple triple centuries in first-class cricket – and would end up with 20s and 30s instead of bigger scores. Now, he sees his batting as an opportunity to make an even greater impact in the match.

However, it is as a 'gun' fielder that Jadeja turns the spotlight on himself. He's electric-heeled, has great hands, terrific anticipation and a fantastic arm that has sent many a batsman to his downfall. Lots of players have speed, grace, catching ability and good throw, but very rarely does one possess all of these. He's the best outfielder I've seen from India, and though he's a natural, his brilliance in the field comes from hours of effort spent in training. When he's not batting or bowling in the nets, Jadeja is with the fielding coach, working on improving his speed and in hitting the stumps directly.

India's dominance at home in the last seven or eight years, apart from runs and centuries scored by top-order batsmen, is primarily because of Ashwin and Jadeja. The country's lineage of spinners is strong, and these two are among the best.

Bishan Singh Bedi, Erapalli Prasanna, Bhagwat Chandrasekhar and Srinivas Venkataraghavan took more than 800 Test wickets between them; Anil Kumble and Harbhajan Singh accounted for over 1,000. Ashwin and Jadeja already have 600-plus. What their final tally will be is anybody's guess, but I wouldn't be surprised if they finish at the top of this pile.

HE'S GOT THE X-FACTOR!

Ben Stokes

In the summer of 2019, Ben Stokes got wide recognition from peers and former players as the world's best contemporary player. His exploits in the World Cup, as well as the Ashes series, where he played the lead role in England's amazing last-gasp victory at Headingley with an incredible undefeated 135, left little scope for debate. What's remarkable is that these performances came on the heels of a major controversy the previous year, when he and Alex Hales were charged with serious misdemeanour following a bar brawl, which almost cost him his career.

If his performance in 2019 brought him to the doorstep of the pantheon of cricket's great all-rounders, by the time the summer of 2020 ended, Stokes had entered the hallowed precinct that boasts outstanding all-rounders. Players like Gary

Sobers, Keith Miller, Richie Benaud, Imran Khan, Ian Botham, Richard Hadlee, Kapil Dev, Andrew Flintoff, Jacques Kallis – that special breed of cricketers who could turn a match on its head with bat or ball in a short spell of time.

In current cricket, Stokes stands unique with his all-round abilities in every format. There are some gifted all-rounders playing today – Ravichandran Ashwin and Ravindra Jadeja from India to name just two – but Stokes has the X-factor that nobody else does.

There are two qualities that separate Stokes from everyone else in his generation. One is supreme fitness. He has a supple body, strong legs and arms, incredible speed as well as lightning-quick reflexes. By themselves, these qualities are enough to make for a fantastic cricketer. What elevates Stokes to a higher category is his great mental strength and remarkable ability to withstand acute pressure, as seen in the 2019 World Cup, the Ashes series after that, and against West Indies and Pakistan in the 2020 home season.

He can play with the derring-do of a Botham and be as unflappable as an M.S. Dhoni in a crisis.

The second facet is more important, and also the more extraordinary considering how Stokes in his early years was chasing controversies with a devil-may-care attitude. In this, he was not unlike a young Ricky Ponting, and almost risked his career. Like Ponting, Stokes too reined himself in to become a formidable talent. It took him longer than the Aussie to sort himself out, and I suppose the T20 World Championship final in Kolkata in 2016, when he was hit for 24 runs by the big Carlos Brathwaite, costing England the title, had something to do with it.

Such an experience can be shattering for any cricketer, especially one who is temperamentally fragile, which Stokes was then. That final took a toll on his cricket, as well as what he did off the field, for which he paid a heavy price. Hats off to the England and Wales Cricket Board for supporting him when he was at his most vulnerable. Cricket Australia had similarly taken care of Ponting. I do wish all cricket boards would treat their young players, especially those with precocious talent, with similar concern and understanding.

Stokes has since repaid the favour and trust shown in him with interest compounded, and in dazzling style. He plays with rare panache, and remarkably, seems to have an ace up his sleeve for all situations, much to the despair of opposing teams.

How long will Stokes's fine run continue, I am often asked. Given the workload on modern cricketers, especially those who play all formats of the game, there is always the threat of injury and burn out. Hopefully, Stokes will be spared that. In which case, I see him scaling even greater heights, for he has guts and determination, and so obviously enjoys success.

WATCH OUT FOR HITMAN

Rohit Sharma

 When it comes to white-ball cricket, there is little doubt that Rohit Sharma will go down as one of the greatest batsmen in the history of the sport. Just past the halfway mark in his career, Rohit has already produced an extraordinary body of work in ODIs and T20s, thanks to his fantastic skills.

He's shown ravenous hunger for runs, hitting three double centuries so far in ODIs, itself a mighty achievement. He dominated the 2019 World Cup, reeling off five centuries – the most by any batsman in a single edition of the tournament. It was unfortunate that despite his brilliance, we stumbled in the semi-final.

True, being an opener is an advantage, since you get to play more overs, but even so, scoring a double century requires more than just time in the middle. It has to do with the batsman's run-scoring capacity. Runs have to be made at a rapid clip, which in turn requires talent, ambition and imagination, a wide range of shots and the ability to improvise.

When in form, nobody in contemporary cricket makes batting look so easy or so pleasing. And in different tenors. One moment he is a sweet, sublime timer of the ball, and the next, he is belting the leather off the ball, sending it over the boundary in different parts of the park.

What makes Rohit so attractive to watch is the way he swiftly adjusts to delivery length, and yet he plays his strokes late, which gives him that split second more to pick what shot to play. He does this unhurriedly, almost effortlessly. Just when you think he is playing a gentle push on the offside, the ball rockets to the boundary, finding the gap between helpless fielders. This breathtaking dimension in his stroke play makes it almost impossible for bowling sides to contain him.

I love watching Rohit bat when he is in top form. Though he is not powerfully built, like a Viv Richards, Gordon Greenidge or Inzamam-ul-Haq, he is a lusty hitter. His shots pack a lot of punch because he is such a splendid timer and is unafraid to loft the ball into the air. When he hits the ball high and long in the V, it's like a golfer teeing off. Some batsmen make run-scoring look an ordeal even when they are a long while in the middle. Rohit makes it look so effortless that you wonder what ails other batsmen who get enveloped in struggle and strife on the same pitch.

The difference is in natural ability: the use of hands, footwork, sense of timing, choice of strokes. He's got a 360-degree range which makes it difficult for bowlers to stop him when he gets going. He is unsparing of pace and slow bowlers, and his improvisations are made to look easy when actually they are fairly complex in execution. Because Rohit is so good, the problem shifts to the fielding side. Unable to stem the flow of runs, they are made to look helpless.

The hallmark of Rohit's batting, however, is technical efficiency. A study of his batting will show that more often than not he is playing terrific orthodox shots. It's just that he plays them with immense control and command. He is, after all, from the 'Bombay School' of batsmanship, but of a modern mindset!

Of all the strokes at his disposal, Rohit's hook excites me the most. This is a high-risk stroke at all times, but he plays it brilliantly, using the depth of the crease to get into a good position, meeting the ball with the sweet spot of the bat, with a perfect swivel giving him the control which lesser batsmen struggle to find.

Brilliant as his record is in white-ball cricket, Rohit wasn't able to do justice to his ability in Test cricket, despite getting off to a flying start. After losing his place in the team, he was finding it difficult to make a comeback, which was obviously playing on his mind. He is a phlegmatic, almost laidback person, but he seemed to be getting restless and frustrated at not making the cut consistently for the five-day format. When I became coach, I sensed the waiting game for opportunities wasn't for him. Moreover, we were losing out on a superb player.

The gauntlet had to be thrown at him. Even in Tests, he could be used as opener, though he had no experience of this in first-class cricket. After discussing this for a while with him, our minds met, and Rohit came through with a superb series as opener against the West Indies in 2019, scoring more than 500 runs.

If he works hard on his fitness, conquers the injuries which crop up every now and then, comes to terms with his own body, puts in the hard yards and settles into a rhythm that allows him to play cricket continuously, Rohit can notch up a Test record which, with his massive achievements in white-ball cricket, would put him in the pantheon of greats.

He's tasted blood as a Test opener, so watch out for the Hitman.

BLOOD, TOIL, TEARS, SWEAT

Virat Kohli

 After Vivian Richards, I haven't seen a batsman dominate as much as Virat Kohli has in the last seven or eight years. He's a consummate cricketer, with excellent technique that facilitates strong defence and possesses a fantastic range of attacking strokes. He also has an irrepressibly positive mindset that sets him apart, and makes him the most prized wicket in the contemporary game.

The turning point in Virat's career came in 2014-15 in Australia. I was Team Director and saw him metamorphose from a talented youngster into a modern great almost overnight. He shifted gears, changed the trajectory of his career with a series of mind-blowing innings and hasn't looked back since.

What makes Virat tick is his unmatched work ethic. In the four decades I've been around, I haven't seen any Indian player work so hard towards excellence. His training and diet regimens have brought a paradigm change in the Indian context. But that is only one part of what makes an outstanding player. Equally important has been his dedication and diligence in constantly trying to improve. In the nets, Virat will spend hours working on minor changes in stance, or the extent of his backlift, when preparing against a team, or even a particular bowler. He does this assiduously for he not only wants to be the best in his own team, but the best against the world's best.

His desire to compete is so intense as to be an obsession. From the outside, some mistake Virat's passion for showmanship, but this is far from the truth. Virat is consistently striving to give himself that extra edge, which in turn can give the team some advantage in the contest. In a way, he's restless – a seeker who is always looking to do new things. Some work, some don't. He takes his learnings and moves on. He thrives on adrenaline and is fired up all time, which some see as effrontery to cricket's etiquette, but he is what he is. Importantly, he never lets his natural aggression conflict with his professional instinct. This makes him an even tougher opponent on the field.

As coach, the great quality I've seen in him is willingness to adapt to specific conditions or the need of the hour. In 2014, Virat was going through a horrible patch in the Test series against England. I was in England too as commentator, and after joining the team as Director for the ODI series, spent quite a lot of time with him. I was amazed to see how positive he was though he was struggling for runs. Forget moping, he was determined and convinced that he would master English conditions soon. Such never-say-die optimism is part of my playbook too and was one of the reasons – apart from believing in the Indian team and the challenge of the task – why I accepted the job of Team Director and later, chief coach. I realized there was an uncut diamond in Virat.

His talent has been evident from his Under-19 days. Early exposure to international cricket can be a double-edged sword. Some players learn even when they fail, some fade away with even minor setbacks. He wasn't a loser, and that made it easier for me. Frankly, the only thing needed for him to succeed consistently was fine-tuning.

Players at the highest level have reached there because they have already put in the hard yards. Coaches should not be giving foundation courses in batting, bowling and fielding at this stage. Any change they recommend should be incremental or subtle. Some players will use this to make gigantic strides, some won't. Progress comes from a player's own discipline, dedication and ambition in constantly setting new personal benchmarks rather than from following advice blandly.

On the field, Virat is totally focused and fiercely competitive. He's in your face, and passionately expressive in whatever he is doing. It may seem like posturing, but it comes naturally to him. India's success over the last five or six years is largely owed to Virat's rapid growth as a champion batsman. He sets the bar high, for himself and others. As a captain, he's matured a lot since taking over from M.S. Dhoni. Unlike MS, who was calm and tranquil in the most difficult circumstances, sizing up opponents and situations astutely and coming up with offbeat moves, Virat's approach is more 'lead-from-the-front'. A draw is only to be considered if victory is impossible. This has rubbed off on his teammates, making India a seriously competitive side playing anywhere now.

Off the field, Virat's a totally different character, very relaxed and chilled out. He wears his superstar status lightly. He enjoys success, of course, but not to the extent that it affects his preparations for the next day or match, or his life off the field. Importantly, he doesn't carry any baggage of the past with him on to the field. He learns from his mistakes, instead of brooding over them, and spends time charging himself up for the next challenge. You might not know what's going on in his mind because he is a perky sort. That can lull opponents into believing that he has dropped his guard. But put him into a contest, and he instantly turns into a bull terrier.

Virat's aggregated runs by the thousands and averages over 50 in Tests, ODIs and T20s, which is a spectacular achievement. His ability to make tall scores in Tests, chase down targets in ODIs and T20s puts him on a pedestal all of his own. His charisma stems from his batting prowess, which reflects his personality. An effervescent stroke player with strong wrists, and a penchant for the pull and drives, there is a distinct element of bottom hand in some of his strokes, particularly the cover drive. But he has worked out for himself how to minimize the risk and how to optimize run productivity.

Bowlers, captains and coaches try to lure Virat into drives that are slightly wide of the off-stump. He's been dismissed on occasion when playing these, but it is not a weakness as some see it. As Ian Chappell always argues, why stop playing strokes that get you plentiful runs just because they can also get you out once in a while?

People often ask me whether Virat and I are kindred souls. I don't know. We are separated by a quarter of a century in age, and have vastly different pursuits, passions and pleasures in life.

Where cricket is concerned, however, our mindsets converge: playing any sport is about self-belief and wanting to win, not settling for being second best.

Virat already has over seventy international centuries, and if he remains fit, he could break all records. He is a master batsman and an entertainer. The runs he makes, and the way he plays, brings in the crowds. He's also become an invaluable ambassador for Test cricket by actively propagating the format. In my opinion, he's the biggest boon to cricket so far this millennium.

ACKNOWLEDGEMENTS

My parents, late Dr Jayadith Shastri and Professor Lakshmi Shastri, both committed and highly successful professionals in their respective fields, for not imposing their views on me, and encouraging me wholeheartedly to follow my passion, often at great cost to their own personal time.

My mama (maternal uncle) Shiva Rao, whose strong artistic streak makes him the odd man out in a family of academics and health professionals. But who, like everyone else in the family, is a diehard cricket lover. That his creative juices are still flowing is evident from the sketches of players used in this book.

Ayaz Memon, journalist of deep knowledge, rich experience and often my harshest critic. We lived on the same street in Mumbai, Mori Road in Mahim, and many years later found ourselves together even in the salubrious countryside of Alibag, a great place to talk cricket. Without his hand-holding, this book wouldn't have been possible.

Alan Sippy, my former Mumbai teammate, a man of considerable 'all-round skills' even in life after cricket. He joined all the dots together to make this project come alive.

And above all, the many cricketers who have enriched my life – personal and professional – in countless ways.

PHOTO 4

Captain Allan Border celebrates after leading his team to victory in the Reliance World Cup final between Australia and England at Eden Gardens, Calcutta, on 8 November 1987. Australia won the match by seven runs. (Photo by Patrick Eagar/Popperfoto via Getty Images)

PHOTO 5

Pakistan's Wasim Akram appeals for the wicket of Derek Pringle during the final of the 1992 Cricket World Cup against England at the Melbourne Cricket Ground. (Photo by Ben Radford/ Getty Images)

PHOTO 6

Indian bowler Anil Kumble being feted by teammates after a perfect ten-wicket haul against Pakistan at the Feroz Shah Kotla ground on 7 February 1999 in New Delhi. (Photo by H.C. Tiwari/*Hindustan Times*)

PHOTO 7

Martin Crowe of New Zealand sweeps for four during the tour match against the Duchess of Norfolk's XI played at Arundel, Sussex on 6 May 1990. New Zealand won the match by seven wickets. (Photo by Adrian Murrell /Allsport)

PHOTO 8

Dennis Lillee and Jeff Thomson at Lord's during the 1975 Cricket World Cup. (Photo by Patrick Eagar/Patrick Eagar via Getty Images)

PHOTO 9

Viv Richards during the India versus West Indies Prudential World Cup final match at Lord's in 1983. (Photo by S&G/PA Images via Getty Images)

PHOTO 10

Indian team manager and Kapil Dev having tea during the third India versus Australia Test match at Sydney Cricket Ground on 2 January 1985. (Photo by Paul Matthews/Fairfax Media via Getty Images)

PHOTO 11

Dilip Vengsarkar of India reacts in the field during the second Test match against England at Feroz Shah Kotla, New Delhi, on 15 December 1984. (Photo by Patrick Eagar/Popperfoto via Getty Images)

PHOTO 12

Sunil Gavaskar batting for India during his 88-run innings in the tour match against Worcestershire at New Road, Worcester, on 29 April 1974. (Photo by Ken Kelly/Popperfoto via Getty Images)

PHOTO 13

Greg Chappell chats with Sourav Ganguly during a practice session at M.A. Chidambaram Stadium in Chennai on 30 November 2005. (Photo by Manan Vatsyayana/AFP via Getty Images)

PHOTO 14

Malcolm Marshall of the West Indies in action during the third Test match against Australia at Queen's Park Oval in Port of Spain on 10 April 1991. The match ended in a draw. (Photo by Ben Radford/Allsport via Getty Images)

PHOTO 15

Sachin Tendulkar in action during a match against Pakistan in Lahore in 1989. (Photo by Ben Radford/Allsport via Getty Images)

PHOTO 16

Surrey batsman Kumar Sangakkara cover drives on day two of the Specsavers County Championship Division One match against Nottinghamshire at Trent Bridge, Nottingham, on 11 April 2016. (Photo by Stu Forster/Getty Images)

PHOTO 17

South Africa's Jonty Rhodes dives during a 1992 Cricket World Cup match against India at Adelaide. (Photo by Patrick Eagar/ Patrick Eagar via Getty Images)

PHOTO 18

England's Graham Gooch salutes the crowds as he reaches 300 runs on his way to score 333 runs against India in the First Cornhill Test match at Lord's in July 1990. (Photo by Bob Thomas Sports Photography via Getty Images)

PHOTO 24

India's Ravi Shastri holds the Man of the Series trophy aloft after the India versus Pakistan, Benson & Hedges World Championship of Cricket final, in Melbourne on 10 March 1985. (Photo by Adrian Murrell/Allsport)

ABOUT THE AUTHOR

Playing sport is about self-belief and wanting to win, and no one knows that better than Ravishankar Jayaditha Shastri.

As a student at Matunga's Don Bosco High School, it was under Shastri's captaincy that the school won the Inter-School Giles Shield in 1977 for the first time. In his final year of junior college at R.A. Podar College, he was selected to represent Bombay in the Ranji Trophy in 1980. Just shy of eighteen, he was then the youngest cricketer to play for Bombay till Sachin Tendulkar arrived.

A year later in 1981, flown in to replace an injured Dilip Doshi, Shastri made his Test debut for India against New Zealand in Wellington. He wasn't even properly kitted and had to borrow manager Polly Umrigar's sweater to fight the bitter cold. He picked up an impressive 6 wickets in two innings, but India went on to lose the match by 62 runs

Just about eighteen months later, Shastri had moved up from number ten in the batting order to opening batsman when India toured England and Sunil Gavaskar was injured. Some months later, he scored his first Test century for India: 128 against Pakistan at Karachi. The same year, he was part of the team that won the ICC World Cup.

The year 1985 was a milestone for Shastri. He made the fastest first-class double century in India playing for Bombay in the Ranji Trophy when scoring runs against Baroda in just under two hours. During the same match, he became the second player in history, after Gary Sobers, to hit six sixes in an over.

The high point of his career came the same year, when he played a major role in leading India to victory in the Benson & Hedges World Championship of Cricket in Australia. For his 182 runs and 8 wickets, Shastri was declared 'The Champion of Champions' and gifted an Audi 100 car. The victory lap with the entire team sitting on the Audi is an abiding memory of India's cricketing excellence.

An opening (or middle-order) batsman and left-arm spinner for the better part of his career, Shastri was an impressive all-rounder, playing 80 Tests and 150 ODIs between 1981 and 1992. The 1988 final Test at Madras against the West Indies marks his only outing as captain. India, trailing 1–0 in the series, beat West Indies by 255 runs to square the series.

Towards the end of the India tour of South Africa in 1992, Shastri found himself grappling with a knee injury. He underwent surgery, which was unsuccessful. In 1994, at thirty-one, he retired from Test and ODI cricket.

His second innings, as commentator, began at the World Masters Tournament in Mumbai in 1995. Sharp observations, punctuated with wit and humour, ensured he quickly became a favourite in the commentary box.

In 2014, Shastri was appointed India's Team Director and, over the next two years, coached the team to Test series wins against Sri Lanka and South Africa. In 2016, India won the Asia Cup T20. In 2017, he was appointed head coach of India.

Credited for building a team with 'a will to win', his term as coach was extended in 2019. Back-to-back wins in Australia – including India's 2–1 series win under the captainship of Virat Kohli in the 2018–19 Border–Gavaskar Trophy and India's historic victory in 2021 – added more feathers to his cap, making him the country's most successful Test cricket coach.

ABOUT THE CO-AUTHOR

 Ayaz Memon is a leading Indian sportswriter, journalist, columnist, author. A qualified lawyer, he chose journalism over legal practice. Rising through the ranks, he has been editor of newspapers like *Mid-Day*, *Bombay Times* and *DNA*, *Sportsweek* magazine and sports editor of the *Times of India* and the *Independent* at different times.

In the course of his four-decades-plus career, Ayaz has covered nine Cricket World Cups, over 200 Test matches and more than 300 ODIs all over the world. He has also been a commentator for Star Sports and Sony, apart from several news channels.

Currently he is a consulting editor at 1Play Sports.

Ayaz has authored the *Wills Book of Excellence: One Day Cricket* and co-authored *India 50: The Making of a Nation* with Ranjona Banerji.

ABOUT THE ILLUSTRATOR

Mumbai resident Shiva Rao is a self-taught artist with a passion for drawing pencil portraits since childhood. Over the years, he has sketched and made caricatures of several film, sports and political personalities.

He is ever grateful to his nephew Ravi Shastri for recognizing his talent and offering him the opportunity to sketch the cricketers featured in this book.